Editor

Brent L. Fox, M. Ed.

Editor in Chief

Karen J. Goldfluss, M.S. Ed.

Creative Director

Sarah M. Fournier

Cover Artist

Diem Pascarella

Art Coordinator

Renée Mc Elwee

Illustrator

Mark Mason

Imaging

Amanda R. Harter

Publisher

Mary D. Smith, M.S. Ed.

Teacher Created Resources
TCR 3656

MW01015215

INSTANT READING COMPREHENSION PRACTICE

- Provides over 240 fiction and nonfiction quick-read activities for applying eight comprehension strategies

- Reinforces reading skills throughout the year

- Includes a "Strategies in Writing" section to practice comprehension skills in an open-ended, short-answer format

- **Correlated to Common Core State Standards**

This is a **tapsponder** enabled resource! See inside back cover for details.

Teacher Created Resources

Authors

Ruth Foster, M. Ed.
Mary S. Jones, M. Ed.

CORRELATED TO COMMON CORE STANDARDS

For correlations to the Common Core State Standards, see pages 141–142. Correlations can also be found at *http://www.teachercreated.com/standards*.

Teacher Created Resources

6421 Industry Way
Westminster, CA 92683
www.teachercreated.com

ISBN: 978-1-4206-3656-7

© *2015 Teacher Created Resources*
Made in U.S.A.

Teacher Created Resources

Table of Contents

Introduction

Instant Reading Comprehension Practice provides short reading and writing exercises that develop and strengthen the skills needed for reading comprehension.

This book is divided into two main sections: *Comprehension Activities* and *Strategies in Writing*. *Comprehension Activities* is divided into eight sub-sections that focus specifically on each of the following comprehension skills:

- Finding Main Ideas
- Noting Details
- Using Context Clues
- Identifying Facts and Opinions
- Finding Cause and Effect
- Sequencing
- Making Inferences
- Predicting Outcomes

Each sub-section includes at least 30 passages with questions designed to challenge students and guide them towards mastery in one of the eight skill areas.

The *Strategies in Writing* section provides students with the opportunity to identify and practice the same comprehension skills but in an open-ended, short-answer format. The activities in this section allow students to focus on a specific strategy and to think more critically as they respond to a given writing task.

A teacher can

- choose to focus on one skill exclusively, going sequentially through the exercises.

- do a few exercises from each skill set to provide daily variety.

- assign specific exercises that will introduce, match, and/or strengthen strategies covered in the classroom.

Writing activities can be assigned at any time and in any order, but each activity focuses on a particular strategy. The strategy is noted at the top of the page. Each strategy has four activity pages, except for *Making Inferences* and *Predicting Outcomes*, which have three each.

Teaching Tips for Specific Exercises

You may want to go through one or two exercises together with the class.

At first, focus on critical-thinking skills rather than speed. Fluency and rate of reading will improve as students practice and gain confidence with each targeted skill.

Remind students that they should read EVERY answer choice. The first answer may sound correct, but there might be a better choice. If they can cross out just one wrong answer, they will have a much better chance of choosing the correct answer.

Finding Main Ideas

Students may find it helpful to sum up what they just read in a short sentence or two before reading the answer choices. Other students may find it helpful to first make a list of three or four key words from the text. Both strategies can help students focus on the most important parts of a passage and not be mislead by incorrect answer choices.

Remind students to choose an answer that covers most of whom or what the paragraph is about. Usually, wrong answers will focus either on details that are too small or too broad. For example, in a paragraph about what bats eat, how they are the only flying mammals, and how they raise their babies, an answer that *only* talks about what bats eat is too "small." An answer that talks about *all* kinds of mammals is too "big." The main idea is bats, not mammals like bears, lions, and porcupines! In other words, students should be thinking, "Not too big, not too small, but just right!"

Pick the correct answer. Students should think about what answer is too big, too small, just right . . . or just wrong!

> You let a thirsty camel drink. The camel has not had water for one week. It has not eaten for a month. Its hump is leaning over and drooping. How much water can the camel drink? It can drink up to 32 gallons!
>
> What is the main idea?
>   **A.** All animals need water to survive. (too big)
>   **B.** The camel has a drooping hump. (too small)
>   **C.** A thirsty camel can drink up to 32 gallons of water. (just right)

Noting Details

Remind students not to panic if they read a passage with a lot of details. They do not have to memorize or remember all the facts and figures! They can always go back and check the passage. Read the following example:

Most of Earth is covered by oceans. The largest ocean is the Pacific Ocean. The second-largest ocean is the Atlantic Ocean. The third-largest ocean is the Indian Ocean.

What is the second-largest ocean?

A. the Pacific Ocean
B. the Atlantic Ocean
C. the Indian Ocean

Answer: B

Ask students if they had to memorize what they read to answer the question or if they went back and looked it up. Point out that all the information they need is still right in front of them and can be reread as many times as necessary.

Using Context Clues

Remind students not to stop reading! Reassure students that they are not expected to know what a word means or what word should go in the blank. They are solving a puzzle! They **must** finish reading the prompt. Then, they can reread the sentence while inserting one of the answer choices into the blank. Usually, they can eliminate choices because some answers will not make sense.

For example, no one expects a child to know the word *defenestrate* (to throw a thing or oneself out of a window). Yet students can correctly choose it if they use the process of elimination, as seen in the following example:

The firefighter had to _____ himself onto a big air pillow when he could not go down the stairs.

What word best completes the sentence?

A. sweep
B. defenestrate
C. bike

Answer: B

Point out that even if they couldn't read the word *defenestrate*, they could cross out and eliminate *sweep* and *bike*. They could still get the right answer!

Identifying Facts and Opinions

Have students ask themselves, "Is this something I think, or do I know for certain?"

Blue flowers are better than orange flowers. If I **think** it, it is an **opinion**.

Some plants have flowers. If it is **certain** or if I can **prove** it, then it is a **fact**.

Finding Cause and Effect

Have students ask themselves, "What happened, and why did it happen?"

What happened is the **effect**. **Why** it happened is the **cause**. If they forget this, students can write **What = Effect** and **Why = Cause** on the top of their page until the information can easily be recalled.

Example: When Sam read the book, he learned that a hippo has a two-foot wide lip!

What happened? (**effect**) Sam learned something. Why did it happen? (**cause**) Sam read a book.

Sequencing

Ask students to read over the sentences in the order students think the sentences happened. Think about what comes first and what comes later. Think about whether the order makes sense. Make sure the last sentence could not have happened until the previous ones did. Consider the following example:

> **1.** Sally started sneezing.
>
> **2.** Sally found a pretty flower on her way to school.
>
> **3.** She picked the flower and smelled it.
>
> What is the correct sequence?
>
> **A.** 1, 2, 3
> **B.** 3, 2, 1
> **C.** 2, 3, 1
>
> *Answer: C*

Making Inferences

When we make an inference, we use **clues** from the story to figure out something the author hasn't told us.

Example: Caesar's heart pounded! He felt a cold trickle of sweat run down his back.

Most likely, was Caesar hungry, tired, or afraid? If Caesar was hungry, it is doubtful that he would be having such a strong physiological reaction. The same logic can be applied to being tired. Being afraid is the only logical answer.

Predicting Outcomes

When we predict an outcome, we make a logical guess about what is going to happen next. Remind students not to answer what happened. They should only be concerned about what might happen in the **future**.

Example: The air was filled with mosquitoes. Lizzie went outside in shorts and a sleeveless shirt.

Have students make logical guesses about what might happen next. (Lizzie gets bitten; she puts on different clothes; she puts on insect repellent, etc.)

Remember: Insist that students read every answer choice! Have them eliminate or cross out the answer choices that don't make sense or that they know are wrong!

Name _____   Date _____

One Big Shoe

Houses can be shaped differently from each other. One house in Pennsylvania is shaped like a shoe. It is called the "Haines Shoe House." It was built over 60 years ago by a shoe salesman. Mahlon Haines built it to advertise shoes. The Shoe House was built near a main road. Now people from all over stop to take a tour.

What is the main idea?

A. People from all over stop at the Haines Shoe House.
B. The Haines Shoe House is a house shaped like a shoe.
C. Houses can be shaped differently from each other.

A Book for Everyone

During a trip to the library, Bob chose a book about trucks. Joshua chose a book about birds. Lisa chose a book about flowers. "Good thing there are plenty of books to choose from," said Bob. Mom was happy to see everyone reading.

What is the main idea?

A. The kids always choose the same books when they are at the library.
B. Mom told all the kids to choose books on different topics.
C. At the library, everyone could find books on topics they liked.

Name _____ Date _____

Summer Plans

It is the last day of school. Eve is sad because she knows she's not going to the same school next year. Her family is moving to a new city over the summer. Near the end of the school day, Eve and her friends exchange phone numbers and addresses. They plan to meet at the county fair next month. Eve is happy that she can still talk to her friends after she moves.

What is the main idea?

   A. Eve is sad that she isn't going to see her friends after she moves.
   B. Eve feels better knowing that she can still talk to her friends after she moves.
   C. Eve is meeting her friends at the county fair over the summer.

A Small Snack

Joe and his two brothers were hungry. They went into the kitchen to make a snack. They all wanted peanut butter on bread. Joe pulled out the bread and the peanut butter. He looked sad when he saw only one slice of bread was left. Joe's older brother said, "Let's share by cutting the bread into three pieces." The brothers all enjoyed their somewhat smaller snack.

What is the main idea?

   A. Joe and his brothers shared a slice of bread for a snack.
   B. Joe's older brother decided to let Joe have his snack.
   C. Joe had a small snack because he wasn't very hungry.

Name _____ Date _____

Don't Bug Me

Sophie used her gift card to buy two toy bugs. The toy bugs crawled around like real bugs. They turned themselves around after bumping into things. Even if the toy bugs got knocked over, they would push themselves up and start crawling again. They looked real. Sophie thought scaring her sister with them would be funny. Sophie's sister screamed so loudly that Sophie never showed the bugs to her again.

What is the main idea?

A. Sophie bought two toy bugs, and they looked very real.
B. Sophie liked to scare her sister over and over.
C. Sophie's sister screams whenever she sees bugs.

Olympic Spirit

Li Duan is an Olympic athlete. Li competes in jumping events in the Paralympics. Before Li jumps, the crowd must be quiet. It is very important for there to be silence. This is so Li and all the other athletes in this event can hear instructions from their guides. Why do Li and the other athletes need to hear their guides? The athletes are blind. They are blind, but they can still jump! With a running start, Li can jump over 40 feet!

What is the main idea?

A. With a running start, Li can jump over 40 feet.
B. All Olympic athletes get instructions from their guides.
C. Li and other blind athletes need silence before they jump in the Paralympics.

Name _____ **Date** _____

Old Friends

It was Tim's first day at his new school. He was nervous because he didn't know anyone yet. After the school bell rang that morning, Tim's teacher had all the students introduce themselves. When Nick introduced himself, Tim smiled. He knew Nick from his other school.

What is the main idea?

   A. Tim felt better after he saw an old friend in his new class.

   B. Tim was not looking forward to going to a new school.

   C. The students in Tim's class introduce themselves every morning.

Happy Campers

Colleen looks forward to going camping in the woods every year. On their trip, Colleen and her family do lots of fun things. They enjoy hiking during the day and roasting marshmallows in the evening. When it gets dark, it is time to go to bed. Colleen rolls out her sleeping bag and places it inside the tent. She thinks it is fun to sleep outside in a tent at night.

What is the main idea?

   A. Colleen thinks it's fun to sleep outside under the stars.

   B. Colleen likes camping because her family does fun activities.

   C. Colleen and her family roast marshmallows in the evening.

Name _____ **Date** _____

Troubled Times

Emma looked up at the smashed clock in horror. She had never thought that the bouncing ball could go up that high. Her mother's favorite clock—broken! Emma liked the clock, too. It had been in the family for generations. Emma fought back tears. How was she ever going to explain to her mother what had happened?

What is the main idea?

   A. Emma must explain why she bounced the ball so high.
   B. Emma's favorite clock was broken.
   C. Emma is upset over a broken family clock.

Yawn Lake

Jake sat on the bench. His shoulders were slumped with boredom. He wondered why so many people were staring at a lake at night. Just then, water started shooting high out of the lake—moving to music! It looked as if the water was dancing. Lights turned on to color the water. It was amazing! "Maybe my parents took me to see something fun after all," he thought.

What is the main idea?

   A. Jake was bored by the nighttime water show on the lake.
   B. Jake was bored until the nighttime water show on the lake started.
   C. Jake was excited about his nighttime trip to the lake.

Name _____ **Date** _____

Science Matters

Matter is anything that takes up space. It can be described by color, size, or texture. Matter comes in three main forms: solid, liquid, or gas. Solids have their own shape, like bricks. Liquids take up the shape of the containers they are in, like water in a cup. Gases, like steam, have no shape and spread out in different directions.

What is the main idea?

A. Matter takes up space and has three forms.
B. Liquids take up the shape of the containers they are in.
C. Matter can be described by color or size.

Fishy Feast

Ben was hiking in Alaska. Ben saw a partially-eaten salmon next to the river. Ben said, "The grizzly bears aren't hungry." How did Ben know if the bears were hungry or not? Salmon swim from the ocean up rivers to lay their eggs. When the salmon first start to swim up the river, the grizzly bears are very hungry. They eat the entire fish. Later, when the bears have eaten their fill of salmon, the bears only eat the most nutritious and fatty parts of the salmon. They eat the eggs, brains, and skins.

What is the main idea?

A. Bears like to eat the eggs, brains, and skins of salmon.
B. Ben was hiking in Alaska next to a river.
C. Ben could tell things about bears from a partially-eaten salmon.

Name _____   Date _____

Secret Recipe

Kate makes the best barbeque sauce in town. Whenever someone asks how she makes it, Kate says, "It's my secret recipe. I put in a little bit of this and a little bit of that until I like how it tastes." All the neighbors want her recipe. Kate often invites them over when she barbeques. The neighbors always come to get a taste of that sauce.

What is the main idea?

   A. Kate gave one neighbor her secret barbeque sauce recipe.
   B. Kate invites some of her neighbors over when she barbeques.
   C. Kate's barbeque sauce is so good that her neighbors want the recipe.

A Day on Two Wheels

Jerry's little brother Seth has been riding a bike with training wheels since he was three years old. Now Seth is five. "I want to take the training wheels off," Seth told Jerry one day. Jerry spent Saturday with Seth teaching him how to ride a bike that doesn't have training wheels. Jerry held the bike while Seth got on it. Balancing the bike was tricky. After a few falls and one or two scrapes, Seth finally figured out how to balance on the bike. Seth finished his first ride just in time for dinner.

What is the main idea?

   A. Seth learned how to ride a bike without training wheels.
   B. Seth wanted to ride his bike, and Jerry told him to be done before dinner.
   C. Jerry told Seth that he will teach Seth how to ride a bike that doesn't have training wheels once Seth is five.

Name _____ **Date** _____

New Stripes

Twenty minutes after Zelda Zebra was born, she could walk. An hour after Zelda was born, she could run. Then, Zelda looked closely at her mother. She memorized her stripe pattern so that she could pick her mother out of the herd. When Zelda was six days old, she saw people for the first time. The people were sitting in the back of a jeep. The people were looking at Zelda and the rest of the herd. Zelda asked her mother, "Without any stripes, how do people know who is who? They all look alike!"

What is the main idea?

   A. Zelda thinks people all look alike.
   B. Zelda did many things before she was one week old.
   C. Zebras have different stripe patterns from one another.

Extra Day to Play

There are 365 days in a year. A leap year is different. If it is a leap year, then the year has 366 days. A leap year happens every four years. The extra day in a leap year is always in the month of February. Instead of 28 days, there are 29. February 29 is called Leap Day. Do you know anyone whose birthday is on Leap Day?

What is the main idea?

   A. In a leap year, another day is added to February.
   B. Each year, Leap Day falls on February 29.
   C. Leap Day birthdays are celebrated every four years.

Name _____ **Date** _____

Cry Baby

Babies need a lot of love and attention. They are unable to do most things by themselves. They can't even dress or feed themselves. They need to be fed and take naps every few hours. When babies need something, they cry to alert others. Someone needs to watch over them all the time.

What is the main idea?

A. The reason babies cry is to alert others.

B. Babies cry every time they have dirty diapers.

C. Taking care of babies requires a lot of work.

Solo Sail

Kay Cottee did something that took her 189 days to complete. Kay did this thing all by herself, and she didn't stop once. Kay was the first woman to sail solo around the world. When Kay was in the Southern Ocean, her boat capsized. Kay was swept overboard. It was a very dangerous and scary time, but Kay was determined to survive. Kay had to struggle, but she got her boat right-side-up, and she got back on board.

What is the main idea?

A. Sailing by oneself is more dangerous than sailing with someone else.

B. Kay was the first woman to sail solo around the world.

C. Kay capsized in the Southern Ocean.

Name _____ **Date** _____

Dirty Water

Water gets polluted in many ways. After you wash dishes or clothes, the used water goes down the drain. The same thing happens when you take a bath or flush a toilet. Factories can make water dirty, too. Used water is called sewage. It must be cleaned before anyone can use it again.

What is the main idea?

  A. Water gets polluted in different ways.

  B. Water gets polluted when you wash dishes.

  C. Water gets polluted in factories.

Bags

The basic backpack has a large storage area and two shoulder straps for carrying it on your back. Some backpacks have only one shoulder strap and are designed to be carried over one shoulder. Other backpacks are on wheels. They have a handle, so you can roll the bag from place to place, just like rolling a suitcase at the airport. Backpacks come in all different shapes, sizes, and colors. What does yours look like?

What is the main idea?

  A. Some backpacks have a handle, so you can roll them from place to place.

  B. Backpacks come in all different shapes, sizes, and colors.

  C. Some backpacks are designed to be carried over the shoulder with one strap.

Name _____ Date _____

Unicorns of the Sea

Narwhals are whales that live in the Arctic Ocean. A narwhal male is best known for the long, straight tusk that grows right through its upper lip. It is a sword-like tooth that can grow up to nine feet long! A female sometimes grows a tusk, but it does not grow as big as the male's. The long tusk gives the narwhal the nickname "unicorn of the sea."

What is the main idea?

A. A male narwhal's tusk grows up to nine feet long.
B. A narwhal's nickname is "unicorn of the sea."
C. A narwhal is a whale best known for its very long, straight tusk.

Two-Wheeled Tour

The Tour de France is a very famous bike race. The race is more than 2,200 miles long. It lasts three weeks! The best cyclists from around the world race in it. The race is split up into smaller races called *stages*. The rider with the fastest overall time after each stage gets to wear the yellow jersey. The winner is the rider who has the fastest overall time by the end of the last stage. The course always ends in Paris, France.

What is the main idea?

A. The race is split up into smaller races called *stages*.
B. The person in first place gets to wear the yellow jersey.
C. The Tour de France is a very famous and very long bike race.

Name _____ Date _____

Pool Party

The movie was about to start. Everyone hurried to jump into the pool. The city was hosting a summer "swim-in" movie night. People were swimming around and floating on different pool toys. The movie played on a big screen that was at the edge of the deep end. Popcorn and drinks were served at the snack table—not in the pool!

What is the main idea?

A. People watched a movie while swimming in the pool.

B. People watched a movie called *Edge of the Deep End*.

C. People hurried to watch a movie on a big screen.

Record Collection

Ashrita Furman likes to set records. Furman even holds a record for having set the most Guinness World Records! Furman holds several mile records. Furman ran the fastest mile while balancing a baseball bat on his palm. He ran the fastest mile with a milk bottle balanced on his head. In less than nine minutes, he ran a mile while balancing a book on his head. Furman also ran the fastest mile while pushing an orange. How did Furman push the orange? He pushed it with his nose! It took Furman less than 23 minutes to push the orange a mile.

What is the main idea?

A. Furman pushed an orange with his nose.

B. Furman can always run a mile faster than anyone else.

C. Furman holds many different Guinness World Records.

Name _____ **Date** _____

Quarter Races

On Mondays, Paul and his older brother Chris sometimes go to the arcade. Games only cost a quarter each on Mondays. The brothers like playing against each other on the racing video games. Some games give out tickets for high scores. Paul and Chris collect their tickets in their pockets. Before going home, they turn them in for prizes that they share.

What is the main idea?

A. Paul and Chris collect their tickets in their pockets at the arcade.

B. Paul and Chris play games together at the arcade and share prizes.

C. Every Monday, Paul and Chris save their quarters for the arcade.

Delicious Accident

Did you know one of the most liked cookies was created by accident? Ruth Wakefield was baking cookies. The recipe called for baker's chocolate. Ruth didn't have any. Instead, she cut up pieces of a chocolate bar. She thought the pieces would melt and mix into the batter. When they didn't, the chocolate chip cookie was born.

What is the main idea?

A. The chocolate chip cookie was created by accident.

B. Ruth Wakefield loves to bake chocolate chip cookies.

C. The chocolate chip cookie is one of the most liked cookies.

Name _____   **Date** _____

Dog Days

Jade wanted a pet. Her parents said she needed to be more responsible. Jade kept her room clean. She did her homework on time, and she helped out with other chores for months. Jade proved she was ready. One morning, her parents took her to an animal shelter. Jade got to adopt the dog of her choice. Jade was thrilled about her newest responsibility.

What is the main idea?

  A. Jade adopted a dog from an animal shelter.

  B. Jade learned to be more responsible in order to have a pet.

  C. Jade's parents told her she needed to be more responsible.

Building a Future

Architects are people who design buildings and create plans for construction. Some architects design small buildings like houses. Some design larger buildings like schools. To be an architect, a person goes to college. He or she takes classes there. These classes teach people how to design buildings and how to draw the blueprints.

What is the main idea?

  A. All architects must go to school for two years.

  B. An architect is a person who designs buildings.

  C. Most architects design houses and schools.

Name _____ Date _____

Bowling Turkeys?

Did you know that turkeys and bowling have something in common? Many years ago, bowling alley owners would give out prizes. The prizes went to people who bowled really well. In the game of bowling, knocking all ten pins down is called a *strike*. Making a strike is very hard. During the week of Thanksgiving, bowling alley owners would give a turkey to players if they could score three strikes in a row. Now, three strikes in a row is called a *turkey*.

What is the main idea?

- **A.** Players try to get a strike during their turn.
- **B.** Bowling alley owners like to give away turkeys.
- **C.** Turkeys and bowling have something in common.

A Long Day

Venus is the second planet from the Sun. Earth is third. Venus is the only planet that rotates backwards. On Venus, the Sun does not rise in the east, and it does not set in the west. On Venus, the Sun rises in the west and sets in the east! Something else is strange about Venus. On Venus, a day is longer than its year! A year on Venus is about 225 Earth days. A day, on the other hand, is 243 Earth days. It takes longer for Venus to make a complete turn on its axis than it does for Venus to go around the Sun!

What is the main idea?

- **A.** In several ways, Venus is not like other planets.
- **B.** A year on Venus is shorter than one Earth year.
- **C.** The sun always rises in the east and sets in the west.

Name _____ **Date** _____

Juice Pops

Isaac had an idea. He got an empty ice-cube tray from the cupboard. He filled each space with apple juice. He then put a toothpick in each space and put the tray in the freezer. The next day, Isaac enjoyed eating his frozen juice pops.

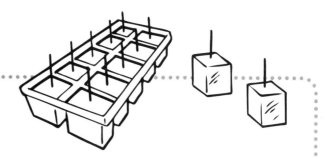

What kind of juice did Isaac use?

  A. grape
  B. orange
  C. apple

Eye Relief

The Larson family has a swimming pool in their back yard. They swim in it about three times a week. Jenny said her eyes hurt after swimming for a long time. Her mom got her goggles. Now Jenny's eyes don't hurt when she swims.

Where does the Larson family swim?

  A. at the beach
  B. in their back yard
  C. at the water park

Name _____ **Date** _____

Car Wash

Tonya and Luke were helping their brother Robert wash his car. Robert drove his car onto the front lawn. He wanted the water to go onto the grass when they rinsed the car. Robert and Tonya scrubbed the car with a soapy sponge. Luke used the hose to rinse the car.

Where was the car parked for the car wash?

   A. in the parking lot

   B. in the street

   C. on the front lawn

Slumber Party

Julie had a slumber party at her house. She invited four friends to come. They played games and read stories. Julie's older sister Gabriella braided each girl's hair. Then they put on their pajamas.

What did the girls do at the party?

   A. They braided each other's hair.

   B. They played games and read stories.

   C. They sang songs and danced.

Name _____ **Date** _____

Halloween Party

Mrs. Hernandez's class is planning a Halloween party. Everyone is signing up to bring something. Some people are bringing paper plates, cups, and napkins. Ethan and Peter signed up to bring fruit. Laurie signed up to bring chips. No one has signed up to bring drinks yet.

Who is bringing fruit?

A. Ethan and Peter

B. Laurie

C. No one has signed up yet.

Faces of Stone

In South Dakota, four giant faces are carved into a granite cliff. The faces are on Mount Rushmore. It took fourteen years to carve the faces. Each face is sixty feet high. The faces are of past presidents. If you face the rock and look directly at it, the face to your left is George Washington. Thomas Jefferson is next to Washington. Theodore Roosevelt is third. Abraham Lincoln is to the far right.

How high is the face of Theodore Roosevelt?

A. 60 feet

B. 140 feet

C. 600 feet

Name _____ **Date** _____

Jogging Club

There is a running track at school. For every lap students run around the track, they earn points for the "jogging club." Jamal's class runs every morning. So far, he has earned the most points in his class.

Where is the running track?

A. at the park

B. at the school

C. at the mall

Fun on the Ice

A new ice-skating rink just opened in Mary's town. She and her family went two weeks after its grand opening. Mary and her sister Rachel each rented a pair of ice skates. Mary's father rented a pair, too. Mary's mother had her own pair of skates. Everyone except Mary knew how to ice-skate. Mary fell a lot, but she still had fun.

Who did not know how to ice-skate?

A. Mary's father

B. Rachel

C. Mary

Name _____ **Date** _____

Box of Goodies

Jim's aunt and uncle offered to bake goodies for a bake sale. That morning, they baked four dozen cookies. They baked two apple pies and two peach pies the next day. Jim's aunt and uncle used a big box to bring everything to the bake sale.

What kind of pies did Jim's aunt and uncle bake?

A. apple and banana

B. apple and peach

C. peach and strawberry

Not Afraid of the Dark

On Sunday evening, the power went out in Joy and Colin's house. Joy and Colin's mom lit many candles and placed them around the house. The family played board games and read stories. They also used flashlights to help them see.

What did the family do?

A. played board games and read stories

B. turned on all the lights

C. went straight to bed

Name _____ Date _____

Blue Tongues

Kyle and Kelly got lollipops after they finished their chores. Kyle and Kelly licked their lollipops. Their tongues turned blue! Kyle and Kelly stuck out their tongues and made funny faces in the mirror.

When did Kyle and Kelly get a lollipop?

A. after they finished their chores

B. after they finished their homework

C. after they finished their dinner

Loving Mothers

Crocodile mothers take really good care of their hatchlings. After they build a nest, the mother crocodile stays close. She guards the nest. She keeps lizards, mongooses, and raccoons from eating the eggs. Sometimes, the mother looks as if she is eating her own eggs. She isn't! She is gently biting them so the hatchlings can get out more easily. She does this only when she hears barking or grunting noises coming from inside the eggs. The hatchlings make this noise when they are ready to break out of the eggs.

The mother crocodile gently bites her eggs

A. before she hears barking or grunting noises inside the eggs.

B. when a lizard, mongoose, or raccoon tries to eat the eggs.

C. after she hears barking or grunting noises inside the eggs.

Name _____ **Date** _____

Accidents Happen

Elena needs a new camera. Her brother Carlos accidentally spilled juice on her old one. Elena wiped it off as well as she could. When she tried to turn her camera on, it didn't work. Carlos said, "I'm so sorry. I didn't mean to do that."

What happened to the camera?

A. Carlos stepped on it.

B. Carlos spilled juice on it.

C. Carlos dropped it in the pool.

Hoop Dreams

Ashley has a large back yard. It has a small basketball court with one hoop. Ashley plays basketball every day. She has become a good player. Ashley now wants to join a basketball team.

When does Ashley play basketball?

A. every Monday

B. every recess

C. every day

Name _____ **Date** _____

Dragon Slayers

Team Dragons was playing Team Knights in the 3:00 p.m. soccer game. Charlie was the goalie for the Dragons, and Stacy was a player for the Knights. Stacy kicked the ball as hard as she could. Charlie tried to block it, but he missed. Stacy scored the first goal for her team!

What are the Dragons and the Knights?

   A. toy names
   B. soccer team names
   C. board games

Ready to Learn

Mia does her homework in the same spot every day. She has a nice desk in her bedroom. It has two drawers. She keeps all her school supplies in them. Mia has everything she needs to do homework at her desk.

How many drawers does Mia's desk have?

   A. two drawers
   B. four drawers
   C. one drawer

Name _____ **Date** _____

Birthday Wish

Luke's dad lit the candles on Luke's birthday cake. Then, holding the cake, Luke's dad walked into the party room, and everyone started singing. Luke wished for a kite. Then, with one breath, he blew out all of the candles.

What did Luke wish for?

A. a car

B. a puppy

C. a kite

A Dragon Among Us

The Komodo dragon is the world's largest living lizard. One dragon was over 10 feet long and weighed 366 pounds! Komodo dragons have a smaller hearing range than humans. Unlike humans, they can't hear high-pitched screams or low-pitched voices. Like snakes, Komodo dragons use their tongues to smell. Komodo dragons like to eat rotting meat. When the wind is right, they can smell rotting meat as far as 2.5 miles away.

How is a Komodo dragon like a snake?

A. They both like to eat rotting meat.

B. They both can hear high-pitched screams.

C. They both use their tongues to smell.

Name _____ **Date** _____

Hooping History

Hula hoops have been around for thousands of years. The ancient Greeks made them from grapevines and used them for exercise. The Greeks didn't call them hula hoops, however. That name came from British sailors. When the British sailors went to the Hawaiian Islands, they saw hula dancing for the first time. The sailors thought the hula dancers moved in the same way people back home did when they were "hooping," or whirling the hoop around their waists.

What did the ancient Greeks call hula hoops?

A. The story does not tell you.
B. They called them exercise grapevines.
C. They called them plastic hoops.

Most Important Meal

Matt always eats cereal with milk for breakfast before school. He has cereal because it is quick to make. For breakfast on weekends, Matt makes either waffles or eggs and bacon. Those take much longer to make.

When does Matt eat waffles?

A. on weekends
B. on weekdays
C. for dinner

Name _____ **Date** _____

Fire!

It was 2:00 in the morning when everyone suddenly woke up. There was a very loud noise. It was the smoke alarm. There was a fire in the kitchen! Someone had left a candle burning. Dad called 9-1-1. Mom helped the kids out of the house. Two minutes later, firefighters arrived in their fire truck to put out the fire. Dad said, "It is a good thing we checked the batteries in our smoke detector last week!"

Who got the kids out of the house?

A. firefighters

B. Mom

C. Dad

Art Appreciation

Kayla won a drawing contest. Her drawing was chosen to be on the cover of her school yearbook. For prizes, Kayla got a free yearbook and a $10 gift card to an ice-cream shop.

What was one of Kayla's prizes?

A. a free yearbook

B. a free ice-cream cone

C. a free drawing

Name _____ **Date** _____

Nature Walk

Dave got a new digital camera. He charged the battery, and the camera was ready to use. Dave and his dad went for a walk. Dave took pictures of plants. His favorite picture was of the Bird of Paradise plant. It has flowers that look like beautiful birds.

When did Dave go for a walk?

  A. after he saw beautiful birds
  B. after he saw the Bird of Paradise plant
  C. after he charged the battery

A Noisy Visit

Lily went to the zoo. First, she visited the monkey house. She liked looking at the howler monkeys. Then she heard a howler monkey howl. It was so loud that Lily had to cover her ears. The zookeeper told Lily that howler monkeys are so loud that their howls can be heard three miles away! Lily visited the reptile house next. The reptile house was very quiet. After looking at the cobras, Lily looked at the pythons.

When did Lily look at the cobras?

  A. before she visited the monkey house
  B. before she looked at the pythons
  C. before the keeper talked to her

Name _____ **Date** _____

Write It Down

Mason wrote a list of foods he wanted to buy from the grocery store. On his list, he wrote: bread, milk, eggs, bananas, lettuce, and grapes. He drew a star next to *bread* because he didn't want to forget it. He also put a star next to *eggs*. His brother needed six for a recipe he was going to try.

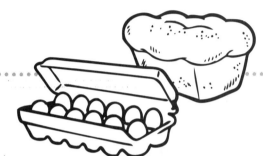

What did Mason write?

A. a menu
B. a recipe
C. a grocery list

Amazing Grace

Grace volunteers at her school library once a month. Each time, Grace spends one hour there after school. She puts books back where they belong. She even vacuums the carpet. Grace enjoys helping the librarian.

How long does Grace stay each time she volunteers?

A. a half hour
B. one hour
C. two hours

Name _____ Date _____

Rough Morning

When Colten woke up this morning, his eyes were very red. They were a little swollen, too. Colten's mother took him to the eye doctor. The eye doctor said that Colten had an eye infection. The doctor gave Colten eye drops to help his eyes heal quickly.

What was wrong with Colten?
- **A.** He couldn't see.
- **B.** He had an infection.
- **C.** He was tired.

Desert Nap

Hannah flew to Arizona to see her grandparents. The flight was four hours long. Hannah fell asleep minutes after the plane was in the air. The lady sitting next to her woke Hannah up when they were landing.

How long was Hannah's flight?
- **A.** four hours long
- **B.** five hours long
- **C.** six hours long

Name _____ **Date** _____

Winter Games

In Drake and Marco's town, it rains almost every day in the winter. On rainy days, Drake likes playing tic-tac-toe. Marco likes playing chess. They like playing games together. When it's not raining, they play outside. They play tag in the park with their friend Ryan. They play baseball in the park, too.

Who likes playing tic-tac-toe?

- **A.** Drake
- **B.** Ryan
- **C.** Marco

Miles of Salt

Around the world there are gold mines and silver mines. There are also salt mines. One salt mine is in Poland. The mine was built about 800 years ago! Salt was mined from it up to the year 2007. The mine is over 178 miles long. It is also over 1,000 feet deep. Miners carved dozens of statues out of salt in the mine. They carved three chapels. They carved an entire cathedral, too. People come from all over the world to go down into the mine. Some people get married in the cathedral. After the wedding, all the guests dance inside the big salt rooms.

How many chapels did the miners carve?

- **A.** dozens
- **B.** 178
- **C.** 3

Name _____ **Date** _____

Moving Pictures

The pictures were placed in a _____ to show what happened first, second, and third.

Which word best completes the sentence?

   A. backwards

   B. cabinet

   C. sequence

Using the Clues

After following the clues with no luck, the answer to the mystery was still _____.

Which word best completes the sentence?

   A. quiet

   B. unknown

   C. amazing

Name _____ **Date** _____

Something to Say

People can _____ in different ways. For example, they can point to things, talk, or write.

Which word best completes the sentence?

A. compete

B. communicate

C. travel

Math Minds

In math, + and – are the _____ used to show addition and subtraction.

Which word best completes the sentence?

A. symbols

B. clothes

C. numbers

Name _____ **Date** _____

Out of Reach

Juana had to _____ her arm as far as she could to reach the cup that was on the top shelf.

Which word best completes the sentence?

  A. wash

  B. bend

  C. extend

Wonderful Water

At times, people can go for weeks without food, but they cannot go without water for that long. At most, a person might be able to go three to five days without water, but it would not be good for you. Water is _____. It is something we need.

Which word best completes the sentence?

  A. essential

  B. amazing

  C. fantastic

Name _____   Date _____

Toy Problem

The problem was finally _____ when the brothers fixed the broken toy.

Which word best completes the sentence?

A. resolved

B. unsafe

C. crazy

Math Helper

Calculators will always give _____ answers when the numbers are entered correctly.

Which word best completes the sentence?

A. false

B. incorrect

C. accurate

Name _____ Date _____

Pick a Number

Alexander was asked for his best _____ as to how many candies he thought were in the jar.

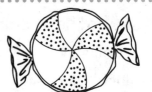

Which word best completes the sentence?

A. writing
B. estimate
C. drawing

A Sad Thought

If there were no more living elephants, the species would be _____ like the dinosaurs.

Which word best completes the sentence?

A. huge
B. extinct
C. scary

Name _____ Date _____

A Favorite Author

After a long _____ about the story, the students wanted to read another book by the same author.

Which word best completes the sentence?

A. flight

B. measurement

C. discussion

Helping Hands

After the hurricane, Joan was amazed at everyone's <u>generosity</u>. People from all over the world wanted to help. They sent water and food. They sent blankets and tents, too. Some people came to help the sick. Others came to help rebuild.

The underlined word means

A. kindness.

B. strength.

C. happiness.

Name _____ Date _____

Pizza Pals

Rick and Liam each ordered a small pizza for dinner. Each pizza was cut into four mini slices. Rick ate three slices. Liam also ate three slices, an <u>equivalent</u> amount to what Rick ate.

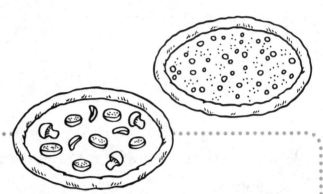

The underlined word means

  A. the same as.

  B. more than.

  C. less than.

Lock It Up

Maria rides her bike to school every day. She always has trouble finding a spot to lock it up in the bike rack. There are always so many other bikes there. One morning, the bike rack was <u>vacant</u>. She wondered why. Then she realized that it was Saturday!

The underlined word means

  A. full.

  B. crowded.

  C. empty.

Name _____   **Date** _____

Fishing for Good Books

Logan grabbed a book from the bookshelf. On the cover, he saw a picture of a man by a lake who was holding a fishing pole. Logan predicted that the book was about fishing. Logan sat down to read it and discovered he was right.

Which word can best replace the underlined word?
- **A.** smiled
- **B.** guessed
- **C.** wrote

Worth Every Penny

Juan had been saving his money for the past year. Juan's mom said he could have a skateboard if he bought it himself. When Juan had enough money, his mom took him to the store. Juan picked out a nice skateboard. It had the kind of wheels that he wanted. Juan felt proud to possess a skateboard that he had bought with his own money.

The underlined word means
- **A.** own.
- **B.** take.
- **C.** give.

Name _____ Date _____

Sweet Sisters

Belle and her little sister Liz like to play together most of the time.
Sometimes Belle likes to play by herself. Sometimes
Liz <u>pesters</u> Belle by poking her in the ear over and
over. Belle does not like that. That's when she
would rather play alone.

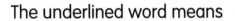

The underlined word means

A. hugs.

B. bothers.

C. colors.

Whale of a Sickness

The boat went up and down on the waves. Ava and James wanted
to see the whales, but the boat's movements were making them feel
<u>queasy</u>. Suddenly, a whale came up next to the boat! Ava and James
were excited. They had never seen anything so big. Looking at the
whale made them forget about
the sick feeling in their stomachs.

The underlined word means

A. hungry.

B. tired.

C. nauseous.

Name _____ Date _____

Mall Madness

Jennifer and her sisters were having a difficult time solving their <u>conflict</u>. Jennifer wanted to go to the toy store, but her two sisters wanted to shop for new bathing suits. They couldn't decide which direction to go.

Which word can best replace the underlined word?

A. problem
B. ending
C. shopping

New Rule

The children at school like to play dodgeball. It's a game in which players try to hit other players with a ball. Today at recess, someone got really hurt in a dodgeball game. After that, the principal <u>declared</u> that there is a new school rule. Dodgeball is no longer allowed at school.

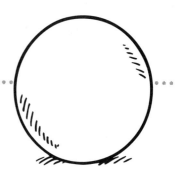

Which word can best replace the underlined word?

A. stated
B. cried
C. laughed

Name _____ **Date** _____

Winning Pies

Did you know Sage won a baking contest? Seven people were in the contest. They had to make the best-tasting pies they could. Sage made blueberry pies. The contest <u>occurred</u> yesterday after school.

The underlined word means

A. counted.

B. cooked.

C. happened.

Well-Prepared

Anne wants to buy a new book bag for the first day of school. She also wants to buy pencils, paper, and pens. Anne has to <u>consider</u> the cost of each item, or else she might not have enough money.

The underlined word means

A. write down.

B. forget about.

C. think about.

Name _____ **Date** _____

Moving West

Neal and his family are moving to a new house. The <u>climate</u> in the area where they live now is very cold. Neal would rather live in a place that is warm all year. Neal is glad that he will no longer need to wear a sweater every day.

Which word can best replace the underlined word?

A. pool

B. weather

C. refrigerator

Snow Blind

What is snow blindness? Snow blindness is like a sunburn to the eyes. It is very painful. Today, people wear goggles to <u>reduce</u> the risk of snow blindness. Long ago, people wore curved bones with tiny slits cut into them. The slits only let in a little of the sun's rays, but they still allowed the person to see.

Which word can best replace the underlined word?

A. increase

B. lower

C. heal

Name _____ **Date** _____

Sunday Football

Henry needed to ask his friends about the <u>location</u> of the park. He wanted to meet them there. Then they were all going to play football together.

The underlined word means

A. time.

B. place.

C. date.

Bugging Out

Whitney needs to <u>magnify</u> a tiny bug. Once she does that, it will be a lot easier to see. She will be able to look at parts she couldn't see before.

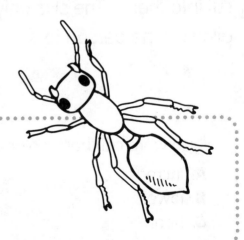

The underlined word means

A. keep the same.

B. make smaller.

C. make larger.

Name _____ **Date** _____

Happy Ending

Jeff wrote a story about a dog that was missing for weeks. In Jeff's story, the dog's owners never found their missing pet. Then, Jeff <u>revised</u> the story's ending. The new ending says that the dog was found a week later and brought back to its home.

Which word can best replace the underlined word?
  A. lost
  B. changed
  C. mailed

Four-Sided Figures

The teacher told me to draw some four-sided <u>figures</u> on the board. I drew a square, rectangle, and diamond.

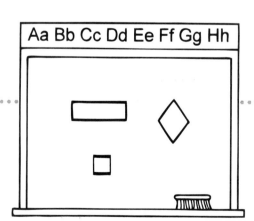

Which word can best replace the underlined word?
  A. numbers
  B. letters
  C. shapes

Name _____ **Date** _____

Friendly Neighbors

The United States is a <u>nation</u>. It has 50 states. It is on the continent of North America. It shares its borders with two countries. Canada is its neighbor to the north. Mexico is its neighbor to the south.

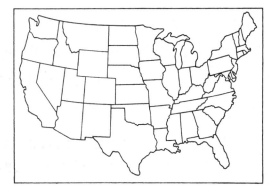

Which word can best replace the underlined word?

A. country
B. state
C. border

Mountain Dreams

Many climbers have the same <u>ambition</u>. They all want to finish the Seven Summits Challenge. The challenge is very hard. Many people fail. What does a climber need to do to take up this challenge? The climber must climb seven specific mountains. He or she must reach the top, or summit, of each mountain. The mountains are all on different continents. Each mountain is the tallest mountain on its continent.

Which word can best replace the underlined word?

A. goal
B. trouble
C. chance

Name _____ **Date** _____

Circle **fact** or **opinion**.

Your Vote Counts!

In the United States, people can vote for their president.
   Is this statement a **fact** or an **opinion**?

Royal Statement

It is better to have a king than a president.
   Is this statement a **fact** or an **opinion**?

Basic Facts

It is much easier to add than to subtract.
   Is this statement a **fact** or an **opinion**?

Math Talk

Take away and *minus* are other words for *subtract.*
   Is this statement a **fact** or an **opinion**?

Four-Year Frenzy

A leap year occurs every four years.
   Is this statement a **fact** or an **opinion**?

Heavy Floaters

Some heavy objects will float when placed in water.
   Is this statement a **fact** or an **opinion**?

Summer Days

The weather is the nicest in the summertime.
   Is this statement a **fact** or an **opinion**?

Just Ask a Teacher

Teachers have the most important job in the world.
   Is this statement a **fact** or an **opinion**?

Name _____ Date _____

Circle **fact** or **opinion**.

Call for Help

In most places, 9-1-1 is an emergency number.
Is this statement a **fact** or an **opinion**?

Big Loop

It takes Earth one year to revolve one time around the Sun.
Is this statement a **fact** or an **opinion**?

Dress to Impress

It is better for students if they wear uniforms to school.
Is this statement a **fact** or an **opinion**?

Fast-Food Critic

Eating food with a plastic fork or spoon ruins the flavor.
Is this statement a **fact** or an **opinion**?

Measuring Up

Centimeters and inches are used to measure short lengths.
Is this statement a **fact** or an **opinion**?

Story Time

Stories about the past are more interesting than stories about the future.
Is this statement a **fact** or an **opinion**?

Sunday, Monday, Funday?

People have the most fun on Tuesdays.
Is this statement a **fact** or an **opinion**?

Happy Teeth

Brushing and flossing your teeth daily will help to maintain healthy teeth.
Is this statement a **fact** or an **opinion**?

Name _____ **Date** _____

A Dime at a Time

Which statement is a **fact**?

    A. Shopping with dollar bills is better than shopping with dimes.

    B. A one-dollar bill and ten dimes are the same amount of money.

Loving Language

Which statement is an **opinion**?

    A. A proper noun is the specific name of a person, place, thing, or idea.

    B. Learning about common and proper nouns is easy.

Word Play

Which statement is a **fact**?

    A. Some words sound the same but have different meanings.

    B. Learning the difference between *to*, *too*, and *two* is tricky.

Extra Butter, Please

Which statement is an **opinion**?

    A. Popcorn is the most delicious snack to eat when you are at a movie theater.

    B. Popcorn is sold at most movie theaters.

Fancy Pants

Which statement is a **fact**?

    A. Blue jeans are too expensive.

    B. Blue jeans come in a variety of designs and sizes.

The Write Stuff

Which statement is an **opinion**?

    A. Authors come up with story ideas very easily.

    B. The person who writes a book is called the author.

For Those About to Rock

Which statement is a **fact**?

    A. Being able to play the drums or the flute is a great skill to have.

    B. People can take classes to learn how to play the drums or the flute.

Name _____   Date _____

Holiday Down Under

Which statement is an **opinion**?
  A. In Australia, January and February are summer months.
  B. The best months to visit Australia are in January and February.

Windy Weather

Which statement is a **fact**?
  A. Hurricane names never start with the letters Q, U, X, Y, or Z.
  B. Hurricanes should not be named in alphabetical order the way they are now.

Bird Sharing

Which statement is an **opinion**?
  A. Ohio should be the only state allowed to have the cardinal as its state bird.
  B. Seven states have the cardinal as their state bird.

Blind Brilliance

Which statement is a **fact**?
  A. There are almost 40 different kinds of dolphins.
  B. The most interesting dolphin is the Indus dolphin because it is blind.

I'll Take the Stairs

Which statement is an **opinion**?
  A. Charles Blondin carried a man on his back and walked across Niagara Falls on a tightrope.
  B. The man Blondin carried on his back across Niagara Falls was braver than Blondin.

Giant Fruit

Which statement is a **fact**?
  A. Movies are always more exciting than books.
  B. The movie *James and the Giant Peach* is based on a children's book.

Summer Splash

Which statement is an **opinion**?
  A. A water park is a great place to cool off on a hot summer day.
  B. For your safety, it is recommended you follow all the rules at the water park.

Name _____ **Date** _____

Practice Makes Perfect

Jayden studied really hard for the math test and <u>got a good grade</u>.

> The underlined phrase is the
>
> **A.** cause.   **B.** effect.

How Rude!

<u>The dog took the ball from the baby</u>, so the baby began to cry.

> The underlined phrase is the
>
> **A.** cause.   **B.** effect.

Baking Smiles

<u>Zoey spent an hour in the kitchen</u> because she had to mix, bake, and frost all the cupcakes.

> The underlined phrase is the
>
> **A.** cause.   **B.** effect.

Hello?

The telephone rang twice, and then <u>I answered it</u>.

> The underlined phrase is the
>
> **A.** cause.   **B.** effect.

Movie Party

<u>Ms. Silver's class was well-behaved all month</u>, so they got to watch a movie.

> The underlined phrase is the
>
> **A.** cause.   **B.** effect.

Name _____ Date _____

Puppy Panic

Rex the dog ran wildly around the yard when <u>he saw a cat go by</u>.

The underlined phrase is the

   A. cause.   **B.** effect.

Too Bright!

<u>It was a very bright day</u>, so Chase wore his sunglasses.

The underlined phrase is the

   A. cause.   **B.** effect.

Time to Relax

Claire pressed "play" on the remote control, and <u>the movie started</u>.

The underlined phrase is the

   A. cause.   **B.** effect.

Nothing to Wear

Dad did laundry because the <u>hamper was full of dirty clothes</u>.

The underlined phrase is the

   A. cause.   **B.** effect.

Just Add Yum!

<u>The milk turned a pretty brown color</u> once Jill stirred in the chocolate powder.

The underlined phrase is the

   A. cause.   **B.** effect.

Name _____   **Date** _____

Too Cool

<u>I wore a sweater to school</u> because it was cold outside.

The underlined phrase is the

A. cause.   **B.** effect.

No Batteries = No Fun

The toy's batteries died because <u>someone left the toy on for hours</u>.

The underlined phrase is the

A. cause.   **B.** effect.

I Can Still See You

<u>The scared hamster wanted to hide</u>, so it went behind a food dish.

The underlined phrase is the

A. cause.   **B.** effect.

Whale-Sized

<u>Max couldn't believe it</u> when he read that a blue whale's tongue can weigh up to 6,000 pounds.

The underlined phrase is the

A. cause.   **B.** effect.

Brain Freeze

Hannah's head started to hurt when <u>she ate a bowl of ice cream too quickly</u>.

The underlined phrase is the

A. cause.   **B.** effect.

Name _____ Date _____

Eight-Legged Race

Four children lined up to run a relay race. When the teacher said, "Go!" Brandon started running. When Brandon finished his lap, <u>he touched Bruce's hand</u>. Then Bruce started to run.

The underlined statement is the **CAUSE**.
What is the **EFFECT**?

   A. Four children lined up.
   B. Bruce started to run.
   C. Brandon ran around the track.

Ice Cold

The water Becca poured from the bottle was not cold. Becca put her cup into the freezer to cool it quickly. Becca forgot that her cup was in the freezer. By the time she remembered, <u>the water had turned into ice</u>.

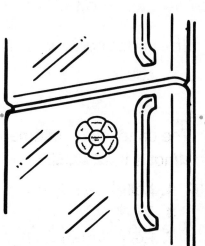

The underlined statement is the **EFFECT**.
What is the **CAUSE**?

   A. Becca put ice into her cup.
   B. Becca wanted to make ice cubes.
   C. Becca left her water in the freezer.

Name _____ **Date** _____

Greedy Gorilla

Nice Newt told Greedy Gorilla that he could have one bag of apples from Newt's tree. Greedy Gorilla put apple after apple into the bag. When Greedy Gorilla was walking home, <u>the bag ripped</u>. All the apples rolled down the street.

The underlined statement is the **CAUSE**.
What is the **EFFECT**?

    A. All the apples rolled down the street.
    B. Greedy Gorilla put apple after apple into the bag.
    C. Greedy Gorilla was walking home.

Bright Flight

It was a very bright day. Kelly heard the sound of an airplane. Kelly looked up at the sky to find it, but <u>she looked away quickly</u> because the sun hurt her eyes.

The underlined statement is the **EFFECT**.
What is the **CAUSE**?

    A. Kelly heard the airplane.
    B. The sun hurt Kelly's eyes.
    C. Kelly started crying.

Name _____ Date _____

No More Dogs

The main choices at the school cafeteria were chicken nuggets and hot dogs. Jason wanted a hot dog for lunch. When he got to the front of the line, <u>no more hot dogs were left</u>. Jason had chicken nuggets for lunch.

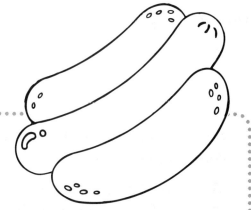

The underlined statement is the **CAUSE**.
What is the **EFFECT**?

   A. Jason didn't want a hot dog for lunch.
   B. Jason had chicken nuggets for lunch.
   C. Jason was glad there were no more hot dogs.

Learning to Tie

April wanted to learn how to tie her shoes. She practiced every day. <u>April finally learned how to tie her shoes by herself</u>. As a reward, April's mom let her buy new shoes that had laces.

The underlined statement is the **EFFECT**.
What is the **CAUSE**?

   A. April practiced tying her shoes every day.
   B. April bought new shoes.
   C. April's mom said she had to learn.

Name _____ **Date** _____

College-Bound

Andrew was a hard-working student. He hoped to learn a lot and earn good grades. <u>Andrew did his homework and read books every day</u>. When his report card came, Andrew was happy to see that he had earned all good grades.

The underlined statement is the **CAUSE**.
What is the **EFFECT**?

   A. Andrew earned all good grades.
   B. Andrew went to the library more.
   C. Andrew didn't want to open his report card.

Helping Hands

The teacher saw Vicky helping a first grader. The first grader had dropped her bag. Vicky was helping the first grader pick up the things that fell out of the bag. No one had asked Vicky to help, but Vicky had stopped what she was doing and had gone over to the first grader. <u>Vicky felt good about what she had done</u>.

The underlined statement is the **EFFECT**.
What is the **CAUSE**?

   A. Vicky dropped her bag.
   B. A teacher saw what Vicky was doing.
   C. Vicky helped a first grader without being told.

Name _____ Date _____

Birthday Surprise

Everyone in the room got quiet. Quinn, the birthday boy, was about to come into the house. <u>"Surprise!" his friends shouted</u> as Quinn opened the door. Quinn was so shocked that his mouth dropped open.

The underlined statement is the **CAUSE**.
What is the **EFFECT**?

   A. Quinn walked into the house.
   B. Everyone in the room got quiet.
   C. Quinn's mouth dropped open.

Summer Spills

An open bottle of sunscreen was sitting by the side of the swimming pool. The wind blew very hard, which made the sunscreen bottle fall over. It landed right on the edge of the pool. <u>A few drops of sunscreen dripped into the water</u>.

The underlined statement is the **EFFECT**.
What is the **CAUSE**?

   A. The open sunscreen bottle fell over.
   B. The water in the pool had to be replaced.
   C. Someone squeezed the sunscreen too hard.

Name _____   **Date** _____

A New Problem

Amber had math problems to do for homework. <u>Amber's pencil broke</u> when she was solving problem number six. Amber looked for a sharpener, but she couldn't find one. Her brother gave her another pencil to use.

> The underlined statement is the **CAUSE**.
> What is the **EFFECT**?
>
>   **A.** Amber sharpened her pencil.
>   **B.** Amber didn't finish her homework.
>   **C.** Amber used another pencil.

Blocked

Miguel and Franklin were playing with blocks. Franklin was stacking the blocks in tall towers. Miguel kept knocking them down, and Franklin did not like that. When their mom saw this, <u>she told Miguel he couldn't play with the blocks anymore</u>.

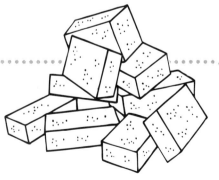

> The underlined statement is the **EFFECT**.
> What is the **CAUSE**?
>
>   **A.** Miguel was being nice to Franklin.
>   **B.** Miguel was throwing blocks.
>   **C.** Miguel was knocking down Franklin's blocks.

Name _____ Date _____

Lunch Bells

Pavlov was a scientist. Pavlov did an experiment with dogs. <u>Pavlov rang a bell, and then he fed the dogs</u>. Pavlov noticed that the dogs began to salivate when they heard the bell. The dogs had learned that the bell meant food!

Robin said, "The lunch bell rang, and now my mouth is watering!"

The underlined statement is the **CAUSE**.
What is the **EFFECT**?

   A. Robin's mouth began to water.
   B. The dogs began to salivate when they heard the bell.
   C. Pavlov was a scientist.

Cooking Up a Plan

Owen and Mindy work together as cooks. They hope to have enough money someday to buy their own restaurant. <u>Owen and Mindy save some money each month to get closer to their goal</u>.

The underlined statement is the **EFFECT**.
What is the **CAUSE**?

   A. Owen and Mindy work together as cooks.
   B. Owen and Mindy need to buy a lot of food.
   C. Owen and Mindy want to buy a restaurant.

Name _____ **Date** _____

Burning Rubber

Natural rubber made shoes and boots waterproof, but it didn't work well. That was because the rubber could not withstand freezing cold or high heat. Then, in 1839, <u>Charles Goodyear accidently dropped a rubber mixture onto a hot stove</u>. Goodyear thought the rubber was ruined. Much to his surprise, his mixture was not ruined. It was weatherproof! It could withstand freezing cold and high heat!

The underlined statement is the **CAUSE**.
What is the **EFFECT**?

   A. It was weatherproof.
   B. It could not withstand freezing cold.
   C. It was ruined.

In the Clouds

<u>Lauren struggled to breathe</u>. She was in the Death Zone. Lauren was climbing Mount Everest. She was above 26,000 feet. At that altitude, the air is too thin for people to survive. There is not enough oxygen. Most climbers use bottled oxygen. Lauren didn't want to use an oxygen tank for her climb. That was why she knew she had to get to the top and back down as quickly as she could.

The underlined statement is the **EFFECT**.
What is the **CAUSE**?

   A. She was below the Death Zone.
   B. She was above 26,000 feet.
   C. She was using bottled oxygen.

Name _____ **Date** _____

Creative Spellers

1. Kathy went next, and she said, "Giraffe."

2. Ms. Sanchez asked the students to name things that start with "j."

3. The teacher reminded her that *giraffe* starts with a "g" and not a "j."

4. Cameron went first, and he said, "Juice."

What is the correct sequence?
   A. 2, 3, 4, 1
   B. 1, 3, 4, 2
   C. 2, 4, 1, 3

Safety First

1. Before crossing the street, stop and look both ways.

2. First, check to see if any cars are driving by.

3. Then wait until the road is clear.

4. Go ahead and cross when you know it is safe.

What is the correct sequence?
   A. 2, 4, 3, 1
   B. 1, 2, 3, 4
   C. 4, 1, 3, 2

Name _____ **Date** _____

New Friends

1. At the end of the school year, Jackson told his parents that he loved his new school.

2. Jackson was nervous on his first day at a new school.

3. Two weeks later, Jackson had made new friends.

4. Jackson had learned where everything was by his third day.

Which sentence comes second?
  A. Sentence 2
  B. Sentence 4
  C. Sentence 1

Crash Course

1. The girl looked at her knee and saw that it was scraped.

2. After she cleaned the scrape, she put a bandage on her knee.

3. The girl was riding her new scooter in the back yard.

4. She tried to go around a chair, but she leaned too far and fell off.

Which sentence comes third?
  A. Sentence 1
  B. Sentence 3
  C. Sentence 4

Name _____   Date _____

Eating like Pigs

1. The farmer poured some food into the pigs' pen.

2. All the pigs ran over to where the food was.

3. The pigs were squealing because they were hungry.

4. The food was all gone within five minutes.

Which sentence comes first?

  A. Sentence 1
  B. Sentence 2
  C. Sentence 3

Ladder Safety

1. Then Caesar asked why the man didn't get hurt when he landed on the hard ground.
2. Caesar liked riddles, so he told Kim about a man who was on a ladder.
3. Kim laughed when Caesar told her that the man had been standing on the bottom step.
4. Caesar said that when the man was on the ladder, he got startled, lost his grip, and fell off.

What is the correct sequence?

  A. 2, 4, 1, 3
  B. 3, 2, 4, 1
  C. 4, 3, 1, 2

Name _____ Date _____

Basement Baseball

1. The picture frame was sitting on top of the bookshelf.

2. Luckily, the glass in the frame did not break.

3. When the rubber ball hit the bookshelf, the frame rocked back and forth.

4. The picture frame fell to the ground.

Which sentence comes second?
  A. Sentence 1
  B. Sentence 2
  C. Sentence 3

Take Me out to the Ballgame

1. The batter swung and hit the ball hard.

2. The batter stared at the pitcher, waiting for him to throw the ball.

3. The pitcher threw the ball as fast as he could.

4. By the time he ran past first base, an outfielder had caught the ball, and the batter was out.

Which sentence comes third?
  A. Sentence 2
  B. Sentence 1
  C. Sentence 3

Name _____ **Date** _____

Too Many Pets?

1. By the time they finished third grade, Dallas and Kendra had a total of three pets.

2. At the end of first grade, Dallas and Kendra got a pet cat.

3. When Dallas and Kendra were in kindergarten, they got a pet dog.

4. After Dallas and Kendra started third grade, they got a pet snake.

Which sentence comes third?
   A. Sentence 4
   B. Sentence 3
   C. Sentence 1

Blowing in the Wind

1. Lots of leaves were on the ground in Charlotte's front yard.

2. Suddenly, the wind blew away the leaves from Charlotte's pile.

3. Charlotte spent fifteen minutes raking up the leaves.

4. Charlotte was upset that she had to rake up the same leaves again.

What is the correct sequence?
   A. 3, 4, 2, 1
   B. 2, 3, 4, 1
   C. 1, 3, 2, 4

Name _____ **Date** _____

A Job Well Done

1. Dylan and his parents opened the report card together.

2. Dylan was so proud when he saw that he had earned good grades.

3. Dylan worked very hard at school to get good grades.

4. When his report card came, Dylan couldn't wait to open it.

What is the correct sequence?
  A. 1, 4, 3, 2
  B. 3, 4, 1, 2
  C. 3, 4, 2, 1

Rubber Chicken

1. They put the chicken bone in a glass of vinegar and waited for three days.

2. The little children gasped in surprise.

3. Lydia and Ely wanted to make a chicken bone bend so they could use it for a trick in a magic show.

4. The children did not think Lydia and Ely's trick would work.

What is the correct sequence?
  A. 4, 1, 2, 3
  B. 3, 1, 4, 2
  C. 1, 2, 3, 4

Name _____ **Date** _____

Fry Guys

1. When they turned golden brown, he took the french fries out of the oil.

2. Raul helped his dad peel potatoes after school.

3. Raul's dad sliced the peeled potatoes into thin strips.

4. He fried the sliced potatoes in hot oil.

Which sentence comes first?
- **A.** Sentence 2
- **B.** Sentence 3
- **C.** Sentence 4

Disappearing Card

1. Brooklyn's mom won the first game, and Brooklyn won the second.

2. When Brooklyn was cleaning up, she counted only twenty-nine cards.

3. Brooklyn was playing a game with her mom that had thirty cards.

4. Brooklyn knew that one card was missing.

Which sentence comes third?
- **A.** Sentence 3
- **B.** Sentence 2
- **C.** Sentence 1

Name _____ **Date** _____

Fighting like Cats and Dogs

1. The big dog saw the cat sitting by the side of the house.

2. The dog sat at the base of the tree and barked at the cat overhead.

3. The dog barked at the cat and started to run towards it.

4. The cat saw the dog coming, so it climbed straight up a tree.

Which sentence comes last?
  A. Sentence 2
  B. Sentence 3
  C. Sentence 4

Snowy Smiles

1. Chloe and Stan skied down the snowy hill in only eight minutes.

2. The friends walked back to the ski lift to go up again.

3. At the ski resort, Chloe and Stan put on snow clothes and skis.

4. Chloe and Stan got on the ski lift that carried them to the top of the mountain.

Which sentence comes second?
  A. Sentence 3
  B. Sentence 2
  C. Sentence 4

Name _____ **Date** _____

Roughing It

1. They began to set up their tent in a flat, open area.

2. They quickly unloaded their things from the car.

3. At noon, the campers arrived at the campsite.

4. When their tent was up, the campers took a walk to the stream.

What is the correct sequence?

   A. 3, 2, 1, 4
   B. 4, 3, 2, 1
   C. 2, 1, 4, 3

Concert in the Kitchen

1. Oscar filled the glasses with varying amounts of water so that the first glass had the most water and the last glass had none.

2. Janna started to sing when she heard Oscar tapping out the tune of "Twinkle, Twinkle, Little Star."

3. Oscar lightly tapped the glasses with a pencil.

4. Oscar lined up eight empty glasses.

What is the correct sequence?

   A. 4, 3, 2, 1
   B. 3, 1, 4, 2
   C. 4, 1, 3, 2

Name _____ **Date** _____

Wrinkle-Free

1. Dad noticed that his work shirt was very wrinkled.

2. Dad plugged in the iron and waited for it to get hot.

3. Now Dad's shirt will look nice when he goes to work.

4. When it was hot enough, Dad ironed his shirt until all the wrinkles were gone.

Which sentence comes first?
   A. Sentence 3
   B. Sentence 1
   C. Sentence 4

Corny Journey

1. The corn was loaded onto a large truck.

2. At the market, the corn was sold at three for one dollar.

3. The farmer harvested the corn from the field.

4. The truck driver drove the corn to a farmer's market.

What is the correct sequence?
   A. 1, 4, 3, 2
   B. 2, 3, 4, 1
   C. 3, 1, 4, 2

Name _____ **Date** _____

Pen Pals

1. Val wanted to write a letter to her friend Amy.

2. She wrote "Your friend, Val" to end her letter.

3. To start the letter, Val wrote "Dear Amy" at the top of the paper.

4. Val then wrote about the fun things she did during her summer break.

Which sentence comes third?
   A. Sentence 1
   B. Sentence 4
   C. Sentence 2

Up and Away

1. While Piper held the kite thirty feet away, Jose held the kite string handle.

2. When the breeze came, Piper threw the kite up into the air.

3. The wind kept the kite up, and Jose slowly let out the string.

4. It was a windy day, so Jose invited his friend Piper to fly a kite with him.

Which sentence comes last?
   A. Sentence 1
   B. Sentence 2
   C. Sentence 3

Name _____ **Date** _____

Running in Circles

1. Aisha and her sister ran around the park, kicking the ball for two hours.

2. Aisha answered, "Let's take the ball and play at the park."

3. Aisha's sister asked, "Do you want to play soccer?"

4. That night Aisha said, "I'm tired from running so much."

Which sentence comes last?

  A. Sentence 4
  B. Sentence 3
  C. Sentence 1

Top-Secret Message

1. When the milk was dry, the paper looked blank, but Brian sent it to Chad.

2. The warm light bulb made the secret message appear!

3. Chad looked at the blank paper, and then he carefully held it close to a warm light bulb.

4. After dipping a toothpick into some milk, Brian carefully wrote a message on a piece of paper.

What is the correct sequence?

  A. 4, 1, 3, 2
  B. 3, 4, 1, 2
  C. 4, 2, 1, 3

Name _____ **Date** _____

Writer's Block

1. Stephanie had been working on her report the entire morning.

2. She called a friend and met him for lunch at the park.

3. They ate sandwiches and shared apple slices.

4. At noon, she decided to take a break from writing.

What is the correct sequence?

A. 1, 2, 4, 3
B. 1, 4, 2, 3
C. 3, 1, 4, 2

Basket of Color

1. The boy didn't know why it looked orange where the apples and pears touched.

2. Then he learned that when red and yellow mix, they make orange.

3. The boy wanted to paint a picture of a basket of fruit.

4. He painted a brown basket filled with red apples and yellow pears.

What is the correct sequence?

A. 3, 4, 1, 2
B. 1, 2, 3, 4
C. 4, 2, 3, 1

Name _____ Date _____

Family Vacations

1. They spent Thanksgiving Day on a flight to Maine.

2. In June, they all went water-skiing at a local lake.

3. The family went camping for Pam's birthday in May.

4. In March, Pam and her parents planned to take three trips together that year.

What is the correct sequence?

A. 3, 1, 4, 2

B. 1, 2, 4, 3

C. 4, 3, 2, 1

The Colors of the Forest

1. Gwen got the four colors she needed out of her crayon box.

2. Gwen's mom gave her a color-by-number page to do.

3. When Gwen was done with the page, it had made a picture of a forest.

4. Gwen colored the 1s blue, the 2s green, the 3s brown, and the 4s yellow.

What is the correct sequence?

A. 2, 3, 1, 4

B. 2, 1, 4, 3

C. 2, 4, 3, 1

Name _____ **Date** _____

Leaf Collection

1. Right after the orange and lemon leaves, Randy put an oak leaf in his notebook.

2. Randy put different pine needles on pages four and five.

3. Last week, Randy began a leaf collection in a notebook.

4. He started off his collection by putting citrus tree leaves at the beginning of the notebook.

Which sentence comes second?

   A. Sentence 4
   B. Sentence 3
   C. Sentence 2

Planetary Positions

1. The sentence helped Leslie because the first letter of each word correctly matches the order of each planet's first letter.

2. Leslie was having trouble remembering the order of the planets.

3. Leslie said, "Now it's easy to remember that the second planet is Venus."

4. Then she thought of the sentence, "My very educated mother just served us noodles."

Which sentence comes third?

   A. Sentence 3
   B. Sentence 2
   C. Sentence 1

Name _____   Date _____

Food Inside

Caleb went inside a large building. In one area, he saw fruits and vegetables. In another area, he saw meats and cheeses. Caleb grabbed a few apples and a pack of string cheese. He took them to a counter where he paid for them. Caleb couldn't wait to eat his snacks.

Most likely, **where** was Caleb?

   A. at a farm
   B. at a mall
   C. at a grocery store

Mommy's Olympian

Tears were running down Nicole's mom's face. Nicole had just won the first-place medal in her school's Reading Olympic Games. Her mother was very proud of her. She knew how hard Nicole had worked at her reading skills. Nicole's mom took a picture of Nicole and her medal. Nicole's mom wanted to frame the picture at home.

Most likely, **how** did Nicole's mom feel?

   A. sad
   B. happy
   C. angry

 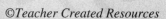

Name _____ Date _____

Best Friends

Sally and Patrick have known each other since they were both two years old. The two friends live right next door to each other. They play at each other's houses every week. If a ball ever goes over the fence from Sally's back yard, Patrick walks home and brings it back quickly.

Most likely, **how** long does it take Sally to get to Patrick's house?

  A. 1 minute
  B. 11 minutes
  C. 1 hour

In Over His Head

Landon and his little brother Evan were at Make Waves Water Park. The first thing they did was go into the wave pool. People in red bathing suits were watching everyone swim. Evan was having trouble swimming in the big waves. A woman in a red bathing suit jumped in to help him. She told Evan to stay at the other end of the pool where the waves were smaller.

Most likely, **who** is the woman?
  A. Landon's mom
  B. a lifeguard
  C. a swimming coach

Name _____ **Date** _____

Star Search

The school talent show is on Friday night. This is a chance for students to show others the special things that they can do. Everyone will be performing on a stage. Some students will play an instrument in the show. Others will dance. Many people are coming to watch the show.

Most likely, **what** will be seen at the talent show?

A. a student coloring

B. a student swimming

C. a student singing

Rocket Girl

Emily always wanted to go to Mars. She wanted to be the first person to step on that planet. She studied for years. She worked hard and became an astronaut. Emily was picked to go to Mars. Emily was in a rocket ship for a long time. Then, Emily landed on Mars. When Emily stepped out onto the planet from the rocket ship, she wore a spacesuit. She could not breathe the Martian air.

Most likely, **how** did Emily feel?

A. thrilled

B. worried

C. disappointed

No Reservation Required

Gabby goes to a restaurant almost every day. She puts on a white coat and makes delicious food. Gabby stays there for hours. People tell her how tasty the food is. This makes Gabby feel very proud.

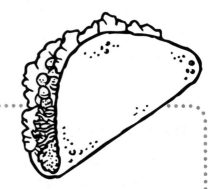

Most likely, **why** does Gabby go to the restaurant?

   A. She works as a cook there.
   B. She loves to eat food from there.
   C. She doesn't like to eat at home.

Not Again!

Tanner had a bad habit of forgetting his math book at school. One day, his teacher told him that he couldn't play at recess if he forgot his book again. Tanner really liked recess time. He didn't want to miss it. Tanner came home from school and sat down to do his homework. When he opened up his backpack, he felt awful.

Most likely, **why** did Tanner feel awful?

   A. He didn't want to do his homework.
   B. He forgot his math book again.
   C. He didn't have any homework to do.

Name _____ **Date** _____

To Grandmother's House We Go

Everyone came over to Grandma's house for a party. People brought food with them. Susan brought mashed potatoes. Daisy brought gravy. Austin brought green beans. Grandma cooked a big turkey. They talked about how lucky they are, and then they ate a great dinner together.

Most likely, **when** was Grandma's party?

A. on Valentine's Day
B. on St. Patrick's Day
C. on Thanksgiving Day

Stay on Target

"Answer the questions on page ten," said the teacher. Everyone in the class started working except for Jane. Jane did not hear the directions. She was too busy drawing pictures. After a few minutes, the teacher asked Jane to give the answer to question one. "What question?" asked Jane. When Jane heard another student giggle, Jane's face turned red.

Most likely, **how** did Jane feel?

A. angry
B. embarrassed
C. mad

Name _____ **Date** _____

Name of the Game

Jordan was dribbling the ball down the court. Suddenly, Mark stole the ball from Jordan and started running to the other end of the court. Jordan ran after him, but he wasn't fast enough. Mark threw the ball and made it in the hoop.

Most likely, **why** did Mark steal the ball from Jordan?

  A. Mark was mad at Jordan and was being mean.
  B. The basketball belonged to Mark.
  C. They were playing basketball against each other.

Chilly Challenge

It was a race to the South Pole. Scott wanted to be first. Scott sailed to Antarctica. Then he left his ship and began to walk. Scott fought the cold and the wind for many days before he came to a tent. There was a flag at the tent. There was a message in the tent, too. The message was from another explorer. It was from Amundsen. Scott was very disappointed.

Most likely, **where** was Scott when he found the tent?

  A. at the South Pole
  B. at the North Pole
  C. close to his ship

Name _____   Date _____

Star Sighting

Zack, Tina, and John were all waiting at the airport. They were going to fly to see their grandparents in New York. A few minutes later, a woman wearing sunglasses sat near them. "Oh, my!" said Tina. "That's the lady from my favorite movie! She plays the funny mom." Tina walked over to tell her how much she liked that movie.

Most likely, **who** is the woman?

 A. an actress

 B. a singer

 C. Tina's friend's mom

Free Ride

Drew wakes up at seven o'clock to start getting ready for school. Drew and his mom leave the house around 7:45 a.m. He sits down and puts on his seat belt. Five minutes later, Drew says goodbye to his mom and then closes the door. He then walks to his classroom from the parking lot.

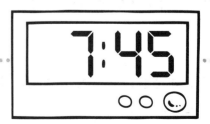

Most likely, **how** does Drew get to school?

 A. He walks with his mom.

 B. His mom drives him.

 C. He rides on the bus.

Name _____ **Date** _____

Homework Helper

Holly had an addition page to do for homework. She used a tool that quickly gave her the correct answers to each problem. All she had to do was press the right buttons and do so in the correct order. Holly showed her dad her answers. Holly's dad said that her answers were all correct. Holly's dad wondered how she had finished the page so fast.

Most likely, **how** did Holly finish the page so fast?

A. Holly did the problems in her head.

B. Holly used a calculator.

C. Holly's dad helped her.

Pizza Man

The one thing Brad likes to eat from the school cafeteria is pizza. Brad buys lunch on Tuesdays because that's pizza day. He takes a lunch from home on the other school days. Two days ago, Brad made a sandwich at home to take for his school lunch.

Most likely, **when** did Brad eat a sandwich at school?

A. on a Sunday

B. on a Tuesday

C. on a Thursday

Name _____ **Date** _____

After-Lunch Activities

The preschool children finished eating lunch. The teachers cleaned the tables and then closed the window shades. Several cots covered the floor. A pillow and a blanket were on each one. The teacher turned off the lights and started to play soft music.

Most likely, **what** were the children going to do?

  A. watch a movie
  B. read a story
  C. take a nap

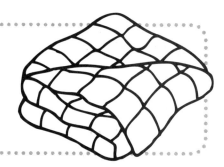

Secret World

The guest speaker said, "One time, while spelunking, I was in danger. My partner and I went down 200 feet on a rope. Then we walked for twenty minutes before coming to a stream of water bubbling up. We put on scuba gear and swam through the water. I got out of the water first. As I was getting out, I dropped my headlight. It was so dark I could not see my hand in front of my face. When my partner came out of the water, she used her headlight to help me find mine."

Most likely, **who** is a spelunker?

  A. someone who explores caves
  B. someone who helps other people
  C. someone who looks for treasure

Name _____ **Date** _____

Birthday Blowout

Troy got a lot of nice gifts for his birthday. He got two new games from his parents. He got gift cards, clothes, and money from other family members. Troy is saving his money for an expensive, new bike. Troy's mom took his birthday money to a place where money is kept safe. When Troy has enough money there, they can take the money out and buy the bike.

Most likely, **where** is Troy's money?

  A. at a bank
  B. in a piggy bank
  C. at a bike shop

Sick Day

Diana got sent home from school because she was sick. Diana's dad picked her up. Then he took her to someone who could help them. A lady in a white coat took Diana's temperature. She looked at Diana's throat, too. The lady said that Diana had an infection. She gave Diana medicine. She told her she could go to school in two days.

Most likely, **who** is the lady?

  A. Diana's mom
  B. Diana's teacher
  C. Diana's doctor

Name _____ **Date** _____

Show and Tell

George's teacher said that anyone with a pet could bring it to school on Friday. George was excited to share his pet Brownie with the class. George brought Brownie in a small glass box. George's teacher was the first to share Max, her pet dog. She showed the class how Max can run and do tricks. Unlike Max, Brownie doesn't have any arms or legs.

Most likely, **what** kind of animal is Brownie?

   A. a hermit crab

   B. a snake

   C. a fish

Painted Butterfly

Linda walked into a school carnival booth that had lots of photos on the wall. She pointed to a picture of a butterfly on the wall. Several minutes later, Linda walked out of the booth with pink wings around her eyes. Linda spent the rest of her time at the carnival playing games. She made three crafts, too. Linda washed the paint off her face as soon as she got home.

Most likely, **how** did Linda get paint on her face?

   A. It came off of one of the crafts she made.

   B. She paid someone who does face painting.

   C. She bumped into a painting of a butterfly.

Name _____ **Date** _____

Far-Away Friends

Wendy's best friend Layla moved to a new state last year. When Wendy was shopping with her mom, she bought a shirt for Layla that said "best friends." Wendy put the shirt in a box and took it to be mailed to Layla. She gave a man Layla's address, and he told her it would arrive in three days.

Most likely, **where** did Wendy take the shirt?

  A. to Layla's house
  B. to the mailbox
  C. to the post office

Free Falling

The wind whipped past Gavin's face. He was hurtling through the air. The ground was coming closer and closer! Gavin was in freefall, and he didn't want to slow down yet. After all, how often does one get to fall to Earth at a speed of over 100 miles per hour?

Most likely, **what** will Gavin do very soon?

  A. slow down before he gets a ticket
  B. get back into an airplane
  C. pull the cord on his parachute

Name _____ **Date** _____

Something for Everyone

The Zipp family all sat down at the table. After looking at the menus, the children ordered a cheese pizza. Mr. Zipp ordered pasta. Mrs. Zipp ordered a salad. Fifteen minutes later, a man brought them their food. He gave them the bill when they finished eating. The Zipp family enjoyed their dinner very much.

Most likely, **where** was the Zipp family?

  A. at a restaurant
  B. in their kitchen
  C. at the school cafeteria

Family Vacation

Allison packed her suitcase. She put in enough clothes for one week. She and her family were going to see the White House for the first time. They all went to bed early because they had to be at the airport first thing in the morning. Allison couldn't wait to start her vacation.

Most likely, **how** did Allison and her family get to their vacation spot?

  A. by train
  B. by plane
  C. by boat

Name _____   **Date** _____

Mixed-Up Meals

Nora has an eating habit unlike anyone she knows. She likes eating breakfast foods but not for breakfast. Nora likes eating lunch and dinner foods for breakfast. Nora's sisters think she's strange. So far today, Nora has eaten pancakes and chicken. She is planning on making bacon and eggs for dinner.

Most likely, **when** did Nora eat pancakes?

- **A.** for breakfast
- **B.** for lunch
- **C.** yesterday

Parent Meeting

Mr. Miller is excited to meet his students' parents. All the students have been working hard in class. Today, Mr. Miller spent hours getting the classroom ready. Now, it is time for the parents to arrive. They are coming to see their children's work and talk to their teacher. Many parents are coming straight from work. Over 30 parents said they would attend.

Most likely, **when** is the parent meeting?
- **A.** right before lunchtime
- **B.** early in the morning
- **C.** in the evening

Name _____   Date _____

Park Pals

Greg goes to school from 8:00 a.m. to 2:30 p.m. on weekdays. He gets out an hour earlier on Fridays. This morning, Greg's friend Steve asked him if he wanted to go to the park. Greg said he would meet Steve at the park around noon. Greg got to the park at 12:05 p.m.

Most likely, **when** did Greg go to the park?

A. on a Saturday
B. on a Wednesday
C. on a Friday

Tiger Tale

Morgan jumped when the tiger roared. The hair on the back of her neck stood up. Morgan could not get over the tiger's huge white teeth. Its body rippled with powerful muscles. Was the tiger looking at Morgan? Morgan wasn't sure, but she stood perfectly still. As she watched the tiger's tail moving back and forth, Morgan was thankful for the strong steel bars.

Most likely, **where** is Morgan?

A. at a zoo
B. in a jungle
C. at a movie theater

Name _____   **Date** _____

Path in the Park

The Cruz family went to the park to ride bikes along the bike path. They packed lunches to take with them. It was a cold and cloudy day. The family enjoyed riding bikes together, but they were still cold. The sun started to come out right before lunchtime. The family knew it would be too cold to sit and eat in the shade. They decided to sit in the sun at a table.

Predict what will happen.

  A. The Cruz family will get colder.
  B. The Cruz family will get warmer.
  C. The Cruz family will buy lunch at the park.

Return to Sender

Jed bought a birthday card to mail to his friend Nam. Jed wrote a nice note to Nam in the card. Then Jed wrote Nam's name, address, and his return address on the envelope. Jed put the card into the mailbox, but he forgot to put a stamp on it. The post office returned the card to Jed because it didn't have a stamp.

Predict what will happen.

  A. Jed will put a stamp on it and mail it again.
  B. Jed will throw the card away.
  C. Jed will ask the post office clerk to send his card.

Name _____   **Date** _____

Picky Eater

Tammie adopted a pet cat from the animal shelter. The lady at the shelter said that the cat likes to eat canned cat food the most. Tammie brought the cat home and tried to feed it dry cat food from a bag. The cat ate one bite and then stopped eating. The cat did the same thing at the next feeding. Then Tammie opened a can of wet food and put it into the cat's bowl.

Predict what will happen.

    A. The cat will only eat one bite of canned food.

    B. The cat will eat all the canned food.

    C. The cat will not eat the canned food.

Scrambled Eggs

Jerome is a good juggler. Yesterday, he juggled three oranges for a minute and never dropped one. Then he started to juggle three raw eggs. Suddenly, Jerome felt as though he had to sneeze. He tried not to sneeze, but he couldn't stop himself. He closed his eyes and sneezed.

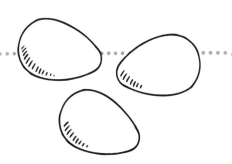

Predict what will happen.

    A. Jerome will blow his nose.

    B. Jerome will eat eggs and oranges.

    C. Jerome will drop an egg.

Name _____ **Date** _____

Toy Shopping

Sarah's mom took her to the toy store. They were buying a gift for Sarah's cousin's third birthday. Sarah's mom said that she had to choose a toy that didn't make loud noises. Sarah found two toys that she thought her cousin would like. One was a wooden alphabet puzzle. The other was a toy fire truck that made loud siren noises when pushed.

Predict what will happen.

A. They will buy the toy fire truck.
B. They will buy the alphabet puzzle.
C. They will buy the fire truck and the puzzle.

Bug Buffet

Jonah went to a "Bug Fair." At the fair, a man told Jonah that many people eat insects. Insects are good to eat because they are cheap and a good source of protein. Then the man offered Jonah some insects to eat. He said Jonah could try a scorpion. He could try fried grasshoppers. He could try a cookie that had crickets in it. Jonah said he wouldn't eat grasshoppers, and he's afraid of scorpions.

Predict what will happen.

A. Jonah will try a scorpion.
B. Jonah will try a grasshopper.
C. Jonah will try a cookie that has crickets in it.

Name _____ **Date** _____

Puppy Party

Every year, Meg's dad puts candles on Meg's birthday cake to match her age. On Meg's eighth birthday, she had a princess party. Her dad put eight princess candles on her cake. Now Meg is turning nine. She is having a puppy-themed birthday party.

Predict what will happen.

   A. Meg's dad will put eight puppy candles on her cake.
   B. Meg's dad will put nine princess candles on her cake.
   C. Meg's dad will put nine puppy candles on her cake.

Game On!

Sean and his friends were playing a board game that they made up. If a player chooses an orange card, he or she moves forward three spaces. If a player chooses a blue card, he or she moves back two spaces. If a player chooses a yellow card, he or she moves forward four spaces. On Sean's turn, he picked a yellow card.

Predict what will happen.

   A. Sean will move forward four spaces.
   B. Sean will move back two spaces.
   C. Sean will move forward three spaces.

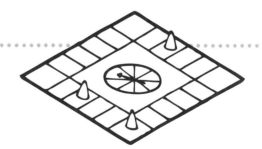

Name _____ **Date** _____

Juice Break

On the shelf in the garage, Brenda found a small bottle of apple juice. She opened it and took one sip. She didn't like the taste of warm apple juice. Brenda put her apple juice into the refrigerator. She said she would drink the juice tomorrow.

Predict what will happen.

   A. The juice will get colder.
   B. The juice will go bad.
   C. The juice will stay warm.

Busy Evening

Ted and Laura always do their chores after school on Thursdays. Their mom says they have to finish their homework before they start any chores. Ted is in charge of taking out the trash. Laura is in charge of vacuuming the living room. They both have to clean their bedroom. Today is Thursday. Both children have homework to do.

Predict what will happen.

   A. The children will start on chores right away.
   B. The children will start on homework right away.
   C. The children will start cleaning their bedroom right away.

Name _____ **Date** _____

A Good Look

Vincent wants to wash his dog. Vincent will need to get his dog all wet. Vincent doesn't want to get wet, but he knows his dog will shake water all over everything. Vincent also knows that a plastic shower cap and rubber gloves will help him stay dry. Vincent laughs at how he looks when he puts on a shower cap and gloves.

Predict what will happen.

  A. Vincent's shirt will get wet.
  B. Vincent's hair will get wet.
  C. Vincent's hands will get wet.

Waxing and Waning

The moon never changes size, but from Earth it looks as if it is getting bigger and smaller. When the moon appears to be getting bigger, it is waxing. When the moon is full, it is big, bright, and round. When the moon looks as if it is getting smaller, it is waning. Ms. Lunar said, "The moon will be waxing for a few more days."

Predict what will happen.

  A. The moon will look as if it is full.
  B. The moon will look as if it is getting bigger.
  C. The moon will look as if it is getting smaller.

Name _____ **Date** _____

Scratch and Sniff

Dana's aunt bought her a pack of scented stickers. Each sticker smelled just like its picture. The smell was stronger when she scratched the sticker first. Dana scratched the banana sticker. It smelled just like a real banana. The strawberry sticker smelled just like a strawberry. Dana scratched the pineapple sticker.

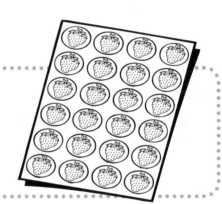

Predict what will happen.

   A. It will smell just like an apple.
   B. It will smell just like a pine tree.
   C. It will smell just like a pineapple.

Low Battery

Ken has a digital camera. It can take many pictures before the battery gets low. When it does get low, Ken has to charge it. Ken was taking lots of pictures at the zoo. Near the end of the day, the "low battery" sign started flashing. Ken took a few more pictures, turned off his camera, and went home.

Predict what will happen.

   A. Ken will take a lot more pictures.
   B. Ken will charge his camera's battery.
   C. Ken will buy a new camera battery.

Name _____   **Date** _____

Sunny Swimmers

Katya is part of a swim team. The team practices in an outdoor pool three times a week. Katya usually puts on sunblock before she jumps into the pool. She uses sunblock, so she does not get burned. Today is swim practice. It is very sunny. Katya was running late today and forgot to put on sunblock.

Predict what will happen.

A. Katya will buy a new bottle of sunblock.
B. Katya will probably not practice with the team.
C. Katya will probably get a sunburn.

No Breakfast

This morning, Blake grabbed his baseball bat and headed towards the door, leaving for baseball practice. His mom shouted, "Wait! You haven't eaten breakfast yet." Blake said that he wasn't hungry yet. He went to baseball practice and came back home three hours later.

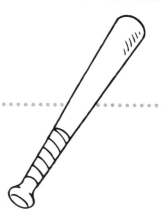

Predict what will happen.

A. Blake will be sleepy when he gets home.
B. Blake will eat lunch at baseball practice.
C. Blake will be hungry when he gets home.

Learning the Letters

The preschool children are learning the alphabet. They learn about one letter each week. They started with the letter *A* the first week. The second week, they learned about the letter *B*. They are going to go in alphabetical order and then start over. Last week, they learned about the letter *J*.

Predict what will happen.

A. They will learn about the letter *C* next week.
B. They will learn about the letter *I* next week.
C. They will learn about the letter *K* next week.

Wolf Packs

Wolves live in packs. Different wolves in the pack have different rankings. Some wolves are "alpha" wolves. They are higher in the social order. Alpha wolves keep their tails high when they meet other wolves in the pack. Lower-ranking wolves will keep their tails hanging down. The lowest-ranking wolves will put their tails between their legs. The scientist watching the wolf pack saw a lower-ranking wolf go up to an alpha wolf.

Predict what will happen.

A. The lower-ranking wolf will keep its tail down.
B. The alpha wolf will keep its tail down.
C. The alpha wolf will keep its tail between its legs.

Name _____ Date _____

Snack Time

The children at Garden Road Elementary School get one snack break and one lunch break every day. Craig had a sandwich, pear slices, and a juice box in his lunch box. He was very hungry during snack break, so he ate half of his sandwich, all the pear slices, and he drank from his juice box.

Predict what will happen.

    A. Craig will have nothing left to eat at lunch.

    B. At lunch, Craig will eat the other half of his sandwich.

    C. Craig will eat another sandwich at lunch.

It's Magic!

Jackie gave Gloria a special marker. Gloria touched the marker with her fingertip, but it didn't leave a mark. "That's weird," she thought. So she tried marking a piece of paper. The marker left a blue line. "That's so cool!" shouted Gloria. "The marker only writes on paper!" Then, Gloria used the marker on her sister's hand.

Predict what will happen.

    A. Gloria's sister will not have a mark on her hand.

    B. Gloria's sister will have a blue mark on her hand.

    C. Gloria's sister will have a red mark on her hand.

Name _____   **Date** _____

Up Too Late

Wu got a new video game as a birthday present. He stayed up three hours past his bedtime playing the new game along with his older brother. The next day, Wu had to get up early for school.

Predict what will happen.

   A. Wu will be very tired.

   B. Wu will get another game.

   C. Wu will play outdoors.

Countdown to Cookies

Tom and Hope wanted oatmeal cookies, so they decided to make some. They mixed the batter and scooped spoonfuls onto a cookie sheet. The recipe said to bake them for twenty minutes. Tom put the cookie sheet into the hot oven for thirty minutes.

Predict what will happen.

   A. Tom and Hope will give the cookies to their friend.

   B. Tom and Hope will sell the cookies.

   C. The cookies will burn.

Name _____ **Date** _____

You're Wearing That?

Shelly woke up early and started getting ready for school. She thought the day was going to be warm, so she put on a pair of shorts and a T-shirt. When Shelly went outside to start walking to school, she got really cold. Then, Shelly went back inside to change her clothes.

Predict what will happen.

  A. Shelly will change into cooler clothes.
  B. Shelly will change into warmer clothes.
  C. Shelly will change into her pajamas.

World Traveler

Noah wanted to see the longest wall in the world. He also wanted to see the deepest lake. Noah knew he would have to go to China and to Russia. When Noah went to China, he saw the Great Wall. Noah liked walking on a wall that was over 1,000 miles long. "Now it is time for me to see Lake Baikal," Noah said. "I can't wait to see the lake that some scientists think is the oldest lake in the world."

Predict what will happen.

  A. Noah will go to Russia.
  B. Noah will go to a lake that is 1,000 miles long.
  C. Noah will walk to the oldest lake.

Name _____ **Date** _____

A Dollar a Day

Angie checked out a book from the library. She has to return it in three weeks. The library charges one dollar for each day that a book is returned late. Angie went to her grandma's house the day the book was due and stayed for the weekend. She didn't return the book until two days after its due date.

Predict what will happen.

A. Angie will have to pay for the book.

B. Angie will not be allowed to check out more books.

C. Angie will have to pay two dollars.

Birthday Cookies

Everyone in Mr. Sing's class is allowed to bring treats to share with classmates on their birthdays. Today is Todd's birthday. He brought cookies so he could share with his classmates. Todd's teacher said Todd could give each student one cookie at recess time. At ten o'clock, the bell rang to start recess.

Predict what will happen.

A. Mr. Sing will keep all of the cookies.

B. Todd will eat all of the cookies himself.

C. Todd will give one cookie to each classmate.

Name _____   **Date** _____

Making Green

Karen was painting a picture of a rose bush. First, Karen painted red roses. While she was painting the leaves, Karen ran out of green paint. Karen didn't want to stop painting. She needed to finish her painting that day. Karen knew she didn't have time to get more paint. Karen knew that blue paint mixed with yellow paint will make green paint.

Predict what will happen.

   A. The leaves in Karen's painting will not all be green.
   B. Karen will paint the leaves with a mixture of blue and yellow paint.
   C. Karen will not be able to finish her painting that day.

Sneezy Sandra

Sandra likes to put pepper on her food. She loves the taste of pepper, but if she uses too much, it always makes her sneeze. Sandra heated a bowl of tomato soup for dinner. She grabbed the pepper shaker, and the lid came off when she shook it. A lot of pepper was in Sandra's soup!

Predict what will happen.

   A. Sandra will sneeze.
   B. Sandra will cry.
   C. Sandra will add salt.

Name _____ **Date** _____

Catching Dinner

The Douglas family went camping for summer vacation. One morning, Mr. Douglas took the children fishing. Mrs. Douglas stayed at the campsite. She said that for dinner she would cook the fish that they caught and heat up some stew. Everyone came back a few hours later. They had caught a total of six fish.

Predict what will happen.
  A. The family will eat only stew for dinner.
  B. The family will eat fish and stew for dinner.
  C. The family will eat dinner late.

Under Water

Bryce heard a boy boast that he could hold his breath underwater for three minutes. Bryce said he could stay "under water" for 15 minutes. Bryce said he could do it without using any air tanks or scuba gear. The boy said it was impossible, but Bryce said he would prove it.

Predict what will happen.
  A. Bryce will fill a glass of water and hold it over his head for 15 minutes.
  B. Bryce will hold his breath for 15 minutes.
  C. Bryce will use air tanks or scuba gear.

Name _____ **Date** _____

The **main idea** of your story is what it is mostly about. If you are writing about George Washington, you don't want to be writing about our solar system!

Below, write five sentences. In each of your sentences, tell what does not go with and what does go with your main idea. The topic of your sentences can be silly or serious. Use the example below as a guide to help you.

Stay On Target

> *Example:*
> *If I were writing about hamsters, I would not write about hurricanes, but I might write about what hamsters eat.*

Make sure you remember to use your commas!

1. If I were writing about _____, I would not write about

_____, but I might write about

_____.

2. _____

_____

_____

3. _____

_____

_____

4. _____

_____

_____

5. _____

_____

_____

Name _____ **Date** _____

An editor is putting together a book about sports. In the book, each chapter is going to be about a different sport. Imagine that your job is to write one of the chapters. First, think of a sport. Think about what you know about it. Then, write one or two paragraphs about the sport.

Best Sports Book Ever

Topics you might want to include:

- an overview of how the game is played
- the object of the game
- rules
- famous players of the game
- your experience with this game (Do you play, watch, or do both?)

Remember to stick to just one sport!

_____

_____

_____

_____

_____

_____

_____

_____

_____

_____

_____

_____

_____

An *autobiography* is a book about a person written by that person. In an autobiography, the author describes facts about his or her own life, actions, and feelings.

My Life as a Shoe

The author will likely use words such as **I**, **me**, **we**, and **us** in an autobiography.

Example:

> When **I** was born . . .
>
> He looked at **me** . . .
>
> **We** walked to the park . . .

You are going to write an autobiography, but first, you are going to have to use your imagination. You are going to imagine that you are a shoe!

Write a paragraph in which you describe what you look like, what happens to you, how you feel, and how you are treated. Remember to use words such as *I*, *me*, *we*, and *us*.

_____

_____

_____

_____

_____

_____

_____

_____

_____

_____

_____

Name _____ **Date** _____

Imagine you are a newspaper reporter. The picture below is part of your story. Think of a caption that can go underneath the picture. The caption should be short and should sum up the action. The caption should fit with the **main idea** of the story.

_____

_____

Now write a paragraph in which you explain more about what is going on in the picture. Use your imagination to fill in details about **where**, **when**, **what**, **why**, and **how**.

_____

_____

_____

_____

_____

_____

_____

_____

Name _____   **Date** _____

Some animals are alike in more than one way. However, similar animals are always different in some ways, too.

Choose two different animals, and then write five sentences about how the animals are *similar* and how they are *different*.

The Same, but Different

> Follow the example below.
>
> *Dolphins and turtles both live in the ocean, but a dolphin doesn't have feet.*

Remember to put a comma before the word *but*!

1. _____ , but

    _____

    _____

2. _____

    _____

    _____

3. _____

    _____

    _____

4. _____

    _____

    _____

5. _____

    _____

    _____

Name _____ **Date** _____

Close your eyes for ten seconds and picture your pet. If you don't have a pet, imagine an animal you would like to own one day.

Now imagine that your pet is lost. You need to write down everything you can about your pet, so it won't be confused with any other pet. When you write, think about its color and size. Also, make sure to include how it feels, how it sounds, what it eats, what it likes to do, and how you can tell it apart from other animals. If you want, you can even include where you last saw it.

LOST PET

_____

_____

_____

_____

_____

_____

_____

_____

_____

_____

_____

_____

Read your paragraph to your classmates, or share it in a small group. Did you provide enough details to keep your pet from getting mixed up with someone else's? Name one detail that makes your pet different from the other pets.

_____

_____

_____

Name _____ **Date** _____

Think of a color. Using only words, how can you describe this color to someone? One fun way is to use a color poem! In your poem, write down details that use our five senses. Describe what your color **looks like**, **sounds like**, **smells like**, **tastes like**, and **feels like**.

The title of your poem should be the color you are describing.

A Rainbow of Possibilities

Red

Red **looks like** a summer sunset.

Red **sounds like** children screaming on a roller coaster.

Red **smells like** a Mexican restaurant.

Red **tastes like** a spicy chili pepper.

Red **feels like** a cool, smooth balloon.

Remember: You can make your color look, sound, smell, taste, and feel like anything you like!

_____ (title)

_____ **looks like** _____

_____ **sounds like** _____

_____ **smells like** _____

_____ **tastes like** _____

_____ **feels like** _____

When you have finished, staple a copy of everyone's poems together to make a book. As a class, decide how the poems should be organized in the book.

Name _____   **Date** _____

Look Closer

Sometimes we need to look closer at a picture to notice all the details. Look carefully at the picture for as many details as you can. Write four details in the spaces below.

1. _____

2. _____

3. _____

4. _____

Now use your details to write a paragraph about what you think is happening in this picture. First talk about the "big picture," and then focus on the smaller details.

_____

_____

_____

_____

_____

_____

_____

Name _____ **Date** _____

Sometimes the writer of a story does not tell you exactly when something is happening. You often need to use clues from what you read to figure out if the story takes place in the past, present, or future.

Traveling Through Time

Write down quotations from three different people from three different time periods. One person will be from the past, one will be from the present, and one will be from the future.

When you are quoting a person directly, make sure you put their words in quotation marks. Your comma goes *inside* the quotation marks.

Example:

"Don't forget to feed the horses," Donna said. "We need them to be strong for our trip to California next week." (Past)

Past:

_____

_____

Present:

_____

_____

Future:

_____

_____

Read one of your sentences to a classmate. Could they figure out whether the person speaking was from the past, present, or future? What words helped them to choose correctly?

_____

Name _____ **Date** _____

It's time to get a little silly! Do you like to make up silly words with your friends? Have you ever told a story using some of these silly words?

Write a paragraph about a vacation or a trip you have taken with your family, but try to use silly, nonsense words to replace some of the real words. Each time you use a nonsense word, make sure you underline it!

Time to Blazamble a Kablookie!

Example:

Last summer, we took a five-hour flight in a <u>fleezbobber</u> because we wanted to relax on the beautiful <u>narfles</u> in Hawaii.

Using the other words in the sentence as clues, what do you think the nonsense words mean?

fleezbobber _____

narfles _____

Now you give it a try!

_____

_____

_____

_____

_____

_____

_____

When you are done with your paragraph, give it to a friend to read. What do they think your nonsense words mean? _____

After returning home from a trip around the world, Jules can't wait to share his vacation photos with you. Unfortunately, Jules doesn't have the best memory. He can't remember where each picture was taken. Can you help him?

Picture Problems

Using at least two clues from each photo, help Jules figure out where he visited on his adventure.

Where was this photo taken?

_____

How can you tell?

• Clue 1: _____

• Clue 2: _____

Where was this photo taken?

_____

How can you tell?

• Clue 1: _____

• Clue 2: _____

Where was this photo taken?

_____

How can you tell?

• Clue 1: _____

• Clue 2: _____

Where was this photo taken?

_____

How can you tell?

• Clue 1: _____

• Clue 2: _____

Name _____ **Date** _____

Two hard words to read are *desirable* and *abominable*.

When something is *desirable*, it is wanted or wished for. It is attractive and desired.

When something is *abominable*, it is horrible or very bad. It is unpleasant or revolting.

Building Your Vocabulary

Imagine you are teaching someone what these two hard words mean. Without stating its definition, write three sentences (six in all) using each word.

Two of the sentences have already been started for you.

1. A *desirable* job would be one that _____

   _____

2. _____

   _____

3. _____

   _____

4. The weather was so *abominable* that _____

   _____

5. _____

   _____

6. _____

   _____

Do you think someone could figure out what *desirable* and *abominable* mean by reading your sentences? How?

_____

_____

Name _____ **Date** _____

A **fact** is a thing that has happened. A fact is true.

An **opinion** is what you think.

Speak Your Mind

Do you have to wear a uniform to school? Do you think you should have to? Why?

Construct a paragraph using facts and opinions to support your answer to the question above.

The **first** sentence starts out like this:

It is a fact that my school (requires/does not require) students to wear a uniform to school. (circle one)

Your **second** sentence starts out like this:

It is my opinion that _____

_____

Sentences **three** and **four** should tell *why* you think so. Give reasons why your opinion is a good one!

I believe this because _____

_____

_____

_____

The **last** sentence should start out like this:

In conclusion, I feel schools across the nation should _____

_____

On a separate piece of paper, combine the sentences from above to form a complete paragraph supporting your opinion.

Name _____ Date _____

Write a dialogue between two children at a zoo. In your dialogue, have each child tell the other at least one **fact** and one **opinion** about what they see during their visit.

Zoo Day

When you write, choose your own names.

Remember to put a colon after the name of the person who is speaking!

Example:

Leif: According to the sign, that snake is over six feet long! *(fact)*

Haley: Yikes! Snakes are the scariest animals on the planet! *(opinion)*

Leif: No way! Spiders are way scarier than snakes! *(opinion)*

Haley: Let's go look at the spiders next. The spider exhibit is located right around the corner. *(fact)*

_____

_____

_____

_____

_____

_____

_____

_____

_____

_____

Pick two classmates to read your dialogue to the class. Have the class identify which sentences are facts and which are opinions.

Name _____ **Date** _____

Is this story true? Write a paragraph in which you explain whether or not this story is factual, and explain why. Make sure you support your answer with **facts**!

Believe It or Not?

I know school buses can fly because I read a book about a school bus that can fly. The flying school bus was yellow, but most school buses are red. My school bus can drive by itself, so there is never an adult on the bus. My bus has four square-shaped wheels filled with water. We line up when we exit the bus through the back window.

_____

_____

_____

_____

_____

_____

_____

_____

_____

_____

_____

_____

_____

_____

_____

_____

_____

Name _____ **Date** _____

A new student who doesn't know how to speak English is coming to your class. You are going to teach this person two new words. These two words will be the only words the person can speak for an entire week! In your opinion, what are the two most important words you can teach this person?

Survival Words

_____   _____

Write a paragraph in which you share what two words you would teach this person, and then explain why you chose these words. Make sure you give examples that support your opinion.

_____

_____

_____

_____

_____

_____

_____

_____

_____

_____

_____

_____

_____

Name _____ **Date** _____

Finding Cause and Effect

Read this sentence:

I was given a small octopus to eat, so I pretended I wasn't hungry.

> *I was given a small octopus* is the **cause**. It is the reason **why** something happens.
>
> *I pretended I wasn't hungry* is the **effect**. It is **what happens** because of the cause.

Practice writing the part of the sentence that is the **cause**.

1. _____, so I ducked behind a tree and stayed as quiet as a mouse.

2. When I _____, I discovered a secret door.

Practice writing the part of the sentence that is the **effect**.

1. After finding a big egg under a pile of leaves, _____

_____.

2. When I put my towel down next to a crab, _____

_____.

Now try to write your own! Make sure your sentence has both a **cause** and an **effect**. Underline the cause. Circle the effect.

_____

_____

_____

_____

_____

_____

_____

_____

Name _____ Date _____

What are some reasons why you might lose electricity in your house?

Lights Out

_____

_____

_____

_____

Write a paragraph in which you first come up with a reason why the power went out. Then, write about some things that might happen due to the power being out. Your paragraph can be realistic, or it can be creative and funny.

_____

_____

_____

_____

_____

_____

_____

_____

_____

_____

_____

_____

_____

_____

Name _____   **Date** _____

Paul Bunyan and Babe the Blue Ox are fictional characters. They are both very large. Folktales have been written about them. In these folktales, what Paul and Babe do has a big effect on the world. Paul makes the Grand Canyon when he drags his axe. Paul makes the Great Lakes when he digs a watering hole for Babe. Mount Hood was made when Paul piled rocks on his campfire to put it out.

Think of a mountain, lake, valley, flat plain, or river. Make up a short folktale about how it was made. Paul and Babe can be part of your folktale if you'd like, or you can create new characters of your own!

You're Not Going to Believe This . . .

_____

_____

_____

_____

_____

_____

_____

_____

_____

_____

_____

_____

_____

_____

Name _____ **Date** _____

Pet Problems

Write a story about a boy or a girl who has a special pet. When the family goes on vacation and leaves the pet at home, the pet sneaks out of the house and starts all kinds of problems around town.

Decide who the owner is and what kind of pet they have. Next, share how the pet escapes from the house, and what happens when it heads into town. Discuss at least two problems that the pet causes, and then share how these problems are solved.

_____

_____

_____

_____

_____

_____

_____

_____

_____

_____

_____

_____

_____

_____

_____

_____

Name _____ **Date** _____

A creature from Saturn comes to visit you. It wants to learn how Earthlings take care of their teeth. You think you did a good job explaining how to properly brush, but instead the creature drinks from the shampoo bottle, sticks a hairbrush in its ear, and then flushes the toilet! You now realize that you must explain in detail what to do. You must give the alien the correct steps in the correct order.

Aliens and Toothpaste

Write down all the steps you must go through to correctly brush your teeth. You may number your steps, or use proper sequencing words such as **first**, **second**, **then**, **next**, **after**, and **finally**.

If you want, you can include small drawings on a separate piece of paper.

_____

_____

_____

_____

_____

_____

_____

_____

_____

_____

_____

_____

Name _____ **Date** _____

Every year at school, you learn more and more things from your teachers and friends. Can you remember some things you learned when you were in kindergarten? How about from when you were in first and second grade?

Look How Much I've Learned

On the lines below, write down something important that you remember learning from each school year. Start with kindergarten and continue up to the third grade.

Make sure you write complete sentences. You can use the examples to help guide you in the right direction.

> *Examples:*
>
> *When I was in second grade, I learned how to _____.*
>
> *I didn't know _____ until I was in second grade.*

Kindergarten: _____

_____

First Grade: _____

_____

Second Grade: _____

_____

Third Grade: _____

_____

Now, write one more sentence about what you hope to learn in the future. Use one of the sentence structures shown below.

> In the future, I hope to _____.
>
> I hope to _____ in the future.

Future: _____

_____

Name _____ Date _____

When you write, these words help the reader to know when things happen:

> **first, second, third, before, previously, then, next, finally, after**

World Traveler

Use at least *five* of these words when you make up a story about traveling around the world. Underline the words you use from the list.

> *Example:*
>
> <u>Before</u> *I was twenty years old, I took a journey around the world. I <u>first</u> drove across North America to visit my home state of Indiana. <u>Second</u>, I . . .*

_____

_____

_____

_____

_____

_____

_____

_____

_____

_____

_____

_____

Name _____   **Date** _____

Look at the pictures. Think about what happened first, second, third, and last. Are the pictures in the correct order? Write a **1**, **2**, **3**, or **4** under each picture to show the correct order. Next, use these pictures to create a story and write a paragraph explaining what happened.

Out of Order

_____

_____

_____

_____

_____

_____

_____

_____

_____

_____

Name _____ **Date** _____

Think of a person, animal, place, or thing.

Next, write down <u>ten</u> sentences about it. Start with the most general. (*For example, "What I am thinking of is alive."*) Give more detailed descriptions as you continue down your list. The last item on your list should be very specific. (*For example, "The animal I'm thinking of has eight tentacles."*)

Narrow It Down

1. _____

2. _____

3. _____

4. _____

5. _____

6. _____

7. _____

8. _____

9. _____

10. _____

What am I thinking about? _____.

Read your list to several classmates. How far on your list did you have to go before someone guessed who or what you were thinking about?

_____

Put a star next to the number each time someone guesses correctly. Which of your classmates needed the least amount of clues?

_____

Name _____ **Date** _____

Think of the many different ways people move around from one place to another. Write down as many modes of transportation as you can think of on the lines below.

Moving Around Town

_____bike_____ _____ _____

_____ _____ _____

_____ _____ _____

Pick three modes of transportation from the list you made above. Then write three complete sentences in which you describe what a person would *do, feel,* or *see* while using one of the words on your list. **Do not reveal your mode of transportation to your readers!** Make them infer it!

Examples:
  1. *I pedaled as hard as I could up the hill.*
  2. *The wheels turned so slowly that I almost fell over!*
  3. *At least I didn't have to worry about my brakes not working!*

Mode of Transportation #1:

  1. _____

  2. _____

  3. _____

Mode of Transportation #2:

  1. _____

  2. _____

  3. _____

Mode of Transportation #3:

  1. _____

  2. _____

  3. _____

Name _____ **Date** _____

A Day in the Life

Some people live very far north. During the winter, they may live for months in total darkness. During the summer, however, the sun never sets. They live in constant daylight.

Imagine that you live in the far north. Write a paragraph about your experiences for one day. First, choose what time of year you are going to write about. Will it be light or dark? Then talk about your day and how you feel. You might want to mention if you do anything special to help you get to sleep, wake up, or keep track of time. Don't say what time of year you are describing! Let the reader figure it out (infer it) from what you wrote!

_____

_____

_____

_____

_____

_____

_____

_____

_____

_____

_____

_____

Name _____   **Date** _____

In the pictures below, you are not told what is going to happen next, but you can come up with some good ideas!

Write down a sentence or two in which you describe the scene. Then, tell what is going to happen *next*.

Use your imagination when you write your sentences, and try your best to entertain the reader!

What Happens Next?

_____

_____

_____

_____

_____

_____

_____

_____

_____

_____

_____

_____

Name _____ **Date** _____

Think of some inventions that have changed the world. Write a few of them on the lines below.

Invention of the Century

_____   _____

_____   _____

_____   _____

Now imagine that you are 30 years old. You have invented something that will change people's lives forever! Write a paragraph in which you describe your invention. Share its name and describe what it does. How is it going to change the world? Be creative! You can invent anything!

Drawing of My Invention

```
┌─────────────────────────────────┐
│                                 │
│                                 │
│                                 │
│                                 │
│                                 │
└─────────────────────────────────┘
```

_____

_____

_____

_____

_____

_____

_____

Name _____   Date _____

Racing Rivals

Two very different athletes are about to compete in a marathon race. The race is more than 26 miles long!

Rich Quickwell

The first runner, Rich Quickwell, is a millionaire who only buys the best running shoes and clothes. He works with a trainer once a week to help him prepare for the race.

Johnny Speedson

The second runner, Johnny Speedson, lives in a small apartment and barely has enough money to buy food. He practices running every night after he gets home from his job. His shoes are falling apart, but it doesn't stop him from trying his hardest and running his fastest.

Imagine that you are a radio newscaster. It is your job to describe the race to people listening on the radio. Before the race begins, introduce both of the runners and predict who you think will win and why. Be sure to make the race sound as exciting as you can, and don't forget to tell who wins!

The beginning of your paragraph has been started for you. Use additional paper if necessary.

Good evening, ladies and gentlemen, my name is _____,

and I'll be your announcer this evening for this very exciting race.

_____

_____

_____

_____

_____

_____

Common Core State Standards Correlations

Each activity in *Instant Reading Comprehension Practice* meets one or more of the following Common Core State Standards (© Copyright 2010. National Governors Association Center for Best Practices and Council of Chief State School Officers. All rights reserved.). For more information about the Common Core State Standards, go to *http://www.corestandards.org* or visit *http://www.teachercreated.com/standards*.

<table>
<tr><td colspan="2" align="center">Reading: Literature</td></tr>
<tr><td>Key Ideas and Details</td><td>Pages</td></tr>
<tr><td>ELA-Literacy.RL.3.1 Ask and answer questions to demonstrate understanding of a text, referring explicitly to the text as the basis for the answers.</td><td>6–13, 17–19, 21–36, 38–50, 55–110</td></tr>
<tr><td>ELA-Literacy.RL.3.2 Recount stories, including fables, folktales, and myths from diverse cultures; determine the central message, lesson, or moral and explain how it is conveyed through key details in the text.</td><td>6–13, 17–19</td></tr>
<tr><td>ELA-Literacy.RL.3.3 Describe characters in a story (e.g., their traits, motivations, or feelings) and explain how their actions contribute to the sequence of events.</td><td>55–80, 96–110</td></tr>
<tr><td>Craft and Structure</td><td>Pages</td></tr>
<tr><td>ELA-Literacy.RL.3.4 Determine the meaning of words and phrases as they are used in a text, distinguishing literal from nonliteral language.</td><td>36, 38–50</td></tr>
<tr><td>Range of Reading and Level of Text Complexity</td><td>Pages</td></tr>
<tr><td>ELA-Literacy.RL.3.10 By the end of the year, read and comprehend literature, including stories, dramas, and poetry, at the high end of the grades 2–3 text complexity band independently and proficiently.</td><td>6–13, 17–19, 21–36, 38–50, 55–110</td></tr>
<tr><td colspan="2" align="center">Reading: Informational Text</td></tr>
<tr><td>Key Ideas and Details</td><td>Pages</td></tr>
<tr><td>ELA-Literacy.RI.3.1 Ask and answer questions to demonstrate understanding of a text, referring explicitly to the text as the basis for the answers.</td><td>6, 8, 11, 13–20, 23, 26, 29, 30, 35, 37–40, 47, 50–54, 65</td></tr>
<tr><td>ELA-Literary.RI.3.2 Determine the main idea of a text; recount the key details and explain how they support the main idea.</td><td>6, 8, 11, 13–20, 23, 26, 29, 30, 35, 51–54, 65</td></tr>
<tr><td>Craft and Structure</td><td>Pages</td></tr>
<tr><td>ELA-Literacy.RI.3.4 Determine the meaning of general academic and domain-specific words and phrases in a text relevant to a *grade 3 topic or subject area*.</td><td>37–40, 47, 50</td></tr>
<tr><td>Integration of Knowledge and Ideas</td><td>Pages</td></tr>
<tr><td>ELA-Literacy.RI.3.8 Describe the logical connection between particular sentences and paragraphs in a text (e.g., comparison, cause/effect, first/second/third in a sequence).</td><td>65</td></tr>
<tr><td>Range of Reading and Level of Text Complexity</td><td>Pages</td></tr>
<tr><td>ELA-Literacy.RI.3.10 By the end of the year, read and comprehend informational texts, including history/social studies, science, and technical texts, at the high end of the grades 2–3 text complexity band independently and proficiently.</td><td>6, 8, 11, 13–20, 23, 26, 29, 30, 35, 37–40, 47, 50–54, 65</td></tr>
</table>

Reading: Foundational Skills	
Phonics and Word Recognition	**Pages**
ELA-Literacy.RF.3.3 Know and apply grade-level phonics and word analysis skills in decoding words.	6–110
ELA-Literacy.RF.3.3.A Identify and know the meaning of the most common prefixes and derivational suffixes.	6–110
ELA-Literacy.RF.3.3.C Decode multisyllable words.	6–110
Fluency	**Pages**
ELA-Literacy.RF.3.4 Read with sufficient accuracy and fluency to support comprehension.	6–110
ELA-Literacy.RF.3.4.A Read grade-level text with purpose and understanding.	6–110
ELA-Literacy.RF.3.4.C Use context to confirm or self-correct word recognition and understanding, rereading as necessary.	6–110

Writing	
Text Type and Purposes	**Pages**
ELA-Literacy.W.3.1 Write opinion pieces on topics or texts, supporting a point of view with reasons.	112, 115, 123, 125, 126, 137, 140
ELA-Literacy.W.3.2 Write informative/explanatory texts to examine a topic and convey ideas and information clearly.	111–112, 114–116, 118, 121–122, 125–128, 131–132, 134, 137, 139
ELA-Literacy.W.3.3 Write narratives to develop real or imagined experiences or events using effective technique, descriptive details, and clear event sequences.	111, 113–114, 116–120, 124, 126, 128–131, 133–140
Production and Distribution of Writing	**Pages**
ELA-Literacy.W.3.4 With guidance and support from adults, produce writing in which the development and organization are appropriate to task and purpose. (Grade-specific expectations for writing types are defined in standards 1–3 above.)	111–140
ELA-Literacy.W.3.5 With guidance and support from peers and adults, develop and strengthen writing as needed by planning, revising, and editing. (Editing for conventions should demonstrate command of Language standards 1–3 up to and including grade 3 here.)	111–140
ELA-Literacy.W.3.6 With guidance and support from adults, use technology to produce and publish writing (using keyboarding skills) as well as to interact and collaborate with others.	117
Range of Writing	**Pages**
ELA-Literary.W.3.10 Write routinely over extended time frames (time for research, reflection, and revision) and shorter time frames (a single sitting or a day or two) for a range of discipline-specific tasks, purposes, and audiences.	111–140

Answer Key

Finding Main Ideas

Page 6
One Big Shoe: B
A Book for Everyone: C
Page 7
Summer Plans: B
A Small Snack: A
Page 8
Don't Bug Me: A
Olympic Spirit: C
Page 9
Old Friends: A
Happy Campers: B
Page 10
Troubled Times: C
Yawn Lake: B
Page 11
Science Matters: A
Fishy Feast: C
Page 12
Secret Recipe: C
A Day on Two Wheels: A
Page 13
New Stripes: B
Extra Day to Play: A
Page 14
Cry Baby: C
Solo Sail: B
Page 15
Dirty Water: A
Bags: B
Page 16
Unicorns of the Sea: C
Two-Wheeled Tour: C
Page 17
Pool Party: A
Record Collection: C
Page 18
Quarter Races: B
Delicious Accident: A
Page 19
Dog Days: B
Building a Future: B
Page 20
Bowling Turkeys?: C
A Long Day: A

Noting Details

Page 21
Juice Pops: C
Eye Relief: B
Page 22
Car Wash: C
Slumber Party: B
Page 23
Halloween Party: A
Faces of Stone: A
Page 24
Jogging Club: B
Fun on the Ice: C
Page 25
Box of Goodies: B
Not Afraid of the Dark: A
Page 26
Blue Tongues: A
Loving Mothers: C
Page 27
Accidents Happen: B
Hoop Dreams: C
Page 28
Dragon Slayers: B
Ready to Learn: A
Page 29
Birthday Wish: C
A Dragon Among Us: C
Page 30
Hooping History: A
Most Important Meal: A
Page 31
Fire!: B
Art Appreciation: A
Page 32
Nature Walk: C
A Noisy Visit: B
Page 33
Write It Down: C
Amazing Grace: B
Page 34
Rough Morning: B
Desert Nap: A
Page 35
Winter Games: A
Miles of Salt: C

Using Context Clues

Page 36
Moving Pictures: C
Using the Clues: B
Page 37
Something to Say: B
Math Minds: A
Page 38
Out of Reach: C
Wonderful Water: A
Page 39
Toy Problem: A
Math Helper: C
Page 40
Pick a Number: B
A Sad Thought: B
Page 41
A Favorite Author: C
Helping Hands: A
Page 42
Pizza Pals: A
Lock It Up: C
Page 43
Fishing for Good Books: B
Worth Every Penny: A
Page 44
Sweet Sisters: B
Whale of a Sickness: C
Page 45
Mall Madness: A
New Rule: A
Page 46
Winning Pies: C
Well-Prepared: C
Page 47
Moving West: B
Snow Blind: B
Page 48
Sunday Football: B
Bugging Out: C
Page 49
Happy Ending: B
Four-Sided Figures: C
Page 50
Friendly Neighbors: A
Mountain Dreams: A

Identifying Facts and Opinions

Page 51
Your Vote Counts!: Fact
Royal Statement: Opinion
Basic Facts: Opinion
Math Talk: Fact
Four-Year Frenzy: Fact
Heavy Floaters: Fact
Summer Days: Opinion
Just Ask a Teacher: Opinion
Page 52
Call for Help: Fact
Big Loop: Fact
Dress to Impress: Opinion
Fast-Food Critic: Opinion
Measuring Up: Fact
Story Time: Opinion
Sunday, Monday, Funday?: Opinion
Happy Teeth: Fact
Page 53
A Dime at a Time: B
Loving Language: B
Word Play: A
Extra Butter, Please: A
Fancy Pants: B
The Write Stuff: A
For Those About to Rock: B
Page 54
Holiday Down Under: B
Windy Weather: A
Bird Sharing: A
Blind Brilliance: A
I'll Take the Stairs: B
Giant Fruit: B
Summer Splash: A

Answer Key (cont.)

Finding Cause and Effect
Page 55
- Practice Makes Perfect: B
- How Rude!: A
- Baking Smiles: B
- Hello?: B
- Movie Party: A

Page 56
- Puppy Panic: A
- Too Bright!: A
- Time to Relax: B
- Nothing to Wear: A
- Just Add Yum!: B

Page 57
- Too Cool: B
- No Batteries = No Fun: A
- I Can Still See You: A
- Whale-Sized: B
- Brain Freeze: A

Page 58
- Eight-Legged Race: B
- Ice Cold: C

Page 59
- Greedy Gorilla: A
- Bright Flight: B

Page 60
- No More Dogs: B
- Learning to Tie: A

Page 61
- College-Bound: A
- Helping Hands: C

Page 62
- Birthday Surprise: C
- Summer Spills: A

Page 63
- A New Problem: C
- Blocked: C

Page 64
- Lunch Bells: B
- Cooking Up a Plan: C

Page 65
- Burning Rubber: A
- In the Clouds: B

Sequencing
Page 66
- Creative Spellers: C
- Safety First: B

Page 67
- New Friends: B
- Crash Course: A

Page 68
- Eating like Pigs: C
- Ladder Safety: A

Page 69
- Basement Baseball: C
- Take Me out to the Ballgame: B

Page 70
- Too Many Pets?: A
- Blowing in the Wind: C

Page 71
- A Job Well Done: B
- Rubber Chicken: B

Page 72
- Fry Guys: A
- Disappearing Card: B

Page 73
- Fighting like Cats and Dogs: A
- Snowy Smiles: C

Page 74
- Roughing It: A
- Concert in the Kitchen: C

Page 75
- Wrinkle-Free: B
- Corny Journey: C

Page 76
- Pen Pals: B
- Up and Away: C

Page 77
- Running in Circles: A
- Top-Secret Message: A

Page 78
- Writer's Block: B
- Basket of Color: A

Page 79
- Family Vacations: C
- The Colors of the Forest: B

Page 80
- Leaf Collection: A
- Planetary Positions: C

Making Inferences
Page 81
- Food Inside: C
- Mommy's Olympian: B

Page 82
- Best Friends: A
- In Over His Head: B

Page 83
- Star Search: C
- Rocket Girl: A

Page 84
- No Reservation Required: A
- Not Again!: B

Page 85
- To Grandmother's House We Go: C
- Stay on Target: B

Page 86
- Name of the Game: C
- Chilly Challenge: A

Page 87
- Star Sighting: A
- Free Ride: B

Page 88
- Homework Helper: B
- Pizza Man: C

Page 89
- After-Lunch Activities: C
- Secret World: A

Page 90
- Birthday Blowout: A
- Sick Day: C

Page 91
- Show and Tell: B
- Painted Butterfly: B

Page 92
- Far-Away Friends: C
- Free Falling: C

Page 93
- Something for Everyone: A
- Family Vacation: B

Page 94
- Mixed-Up Meals: B
- Parent Meeting: C

Page 95
- Park Pals: A
- Tiger Tale: A

Predicting Outcomes
Page 96
- Path in the Park: B
- Return to Sender: A

Page 97
- Picky Eater: B
- Scrambled Eggs: C

Page 98
- Toy Shopping: B
- Bug Buffet: C

Page 99
- Puppy Party: C
- Game On!: A

Page 100
- Juice Break: A
- Busy Evening: B

Page 101
- A Good Look: A
- Waxing and Waning: B

Page 102
- Scratch and Sniff: C
- Low Battery: B

Page 103
- Sunny Swimmers: C
- No Breakfast: C

Page 104
- Learning the Letters: C
- Wolf Packs: A

Page 105
- Snack Time: B
- It's Magic!: A

Page 106
- Up Too Late: A
- Countdown to Cookies: C

Page 107
- You're Wearing That?: B
- World Traveler: A

Page 108
- A Dollar a Day: C
- Birthday Cookies: C

Page 109
- Making Green: B
- Sneezy Sandra: A

Page 110
- Catching Dinner: B
- Under Water: A

#3656 Instant Reading Comprehension Practice   144   ©*Teacher Created Resources*